Your *Kids*

Their Lives

a parent's
guide
to raising
happy,
competent,
caring
children

MALINDA JO MUZI

PINK
ROSES
PUBLISHING
Merion Station, PA

YOUR KIDS, THEIR LIVES:
A Parent's Guide to Raising Happy, Competent, Caring Children
Malinda Jo Muzi

Published by:
Pink Roses Publishing
PO Box 307
Merion Station, PA 19066-1019
Orders@PinkRosesPublishing.com

http://www.PinkRosesPublishing.com
All rights reserved
Copyright © 2006 by Malinda Jo Muzi

Publisher's Cataloging-in-Publication Data
Muzi, Malinda Jo 1942–
  YOUR KIDS, THEIR LIVES:
  A Parent's Guide to Raising Happy, Competent, Caring Children
  by Malinda Jo Muzi

ISBN: 0-9776969-0-1

1. parent and child 2. parenting 3. family dynamics 4. discipline
5. child rearing 6. parent-child communication
7. parent-child attachment

Library of Congress Control Number: 2006903035

Jacket Design: ATG Productions, LLC, Christy Moeller-Masel, Phoenix, Arizona
Book Design & Typesetting: ATG Productions, LLC, Cory Olson, Surprise, Arizona
Printing: Freisens, Altona, Manitoba, Canada

Printed and bound in Canada

For Marcia Epstein

...we need not reinforce ourselves, or send
tokens of rememberance: I rely on (her) as on myself:
if (she) did thus or thus, I know it was right.

Ralph Waldo Emerson

Also by Malinda Jo Muzi

Psychology: A Biographical Approach
Child Development Through Time and Transition
The Experience of Parenting

ACKNOWLEDGEMENTS

Shakespeare wrote that ingratitude is a worse offense than lying, vainness or babbling drunkenness. With this in mind I want to express my appreciation to the people who made this book and my writing life possible.

Wen Potter's ideas and editing helped shape the book and moved it forward whenever it got too long-winded and detailed.

In a stroke of good fortune I found Kelly Scott-Olson of ATG Productions, and happily turned the life of the book over to her after the writing was completed. Kelly's design team made the book come alive, particularly Christy Moeller-Masel's beautiful cover and Cory Olson's brisk interior design.

I am grateful to my son Jarrett, who has been supportive of my writing since he first got familiar with take-out dinners as a little boy.

There are not enough ways to thank Ann Angelone, Barbara and Barry Sirkin, Lea Zacharka, Janet Fetkewicz and Rick Shugart for their company and caring during the writing of this book. A special appreciation to the Castelluci's—Judy, Paul, Theresa and Paulie—for making my life easier and wonderful.

My writing life would be far more solitary than it is without Elliott. His presence means coffee is made, the doorbell is answered, the dogs and cats are fed, and there is someone to hold hands with, talk to and laugh with at the end of a long working day.

TABLE OF CONTENTS

Chapter One   Restless Ghosts 16

Chapter Two   Being and Doing 20

Chapter Three   Guess Who's Coming Forever? 25

Chapter Four   Invitation to a Dance 33

Chapter Five   Balancing Act 44

Chapter Six   Parents As Soothsayers 58

Chapter Seven   Hearth and Home 67

Chapter Eight   Change and Challenge 96

Chapter Nine   The Social Contract 113

Chapter Ten   Letting Go and Holding On 124

Chapter Eleven   You Can't Take Back the Wind 152

Chapter Twelve   Teaching Children Well 169

Chapter Thirteen   Restless Ghosts Revisited 202

INTRODUCTION

Most of today's mothers and fathers are caring and concerned parents, looking for the best possible advice to help them raise happy, competent, caring children. In hopes of accomplishing this they turn for guidance to family physicians, family members, television personalities, newspaper columnists, advice books and the lady down the street who has five kids and they all seem normal. Because parents worry, the subject of parenting is big business in America. Entire magazines are devoted to child rearing issues. Bookstore shelves are filled with treatises on topics ranging from toilet training in less than a day (as if this is important to accomplish), to play therapy (just in case toilet training in less than a day doesn't work out.) Newspapers throughout the country assign columnists to the subject. Cable networks offer advice on contemporary issues of raising children, and television talk show hosts fill endless hours debating parenting methods and techniques.

Unfortunately, much of the counsel offered to parents is based upon subjective opinion, conjecture, and the personal background, beliefs and attitudes of the "expert" making the recommendations. Instructions are generally narrow and often constructed on little or no scientific evidence. While some of the counsel presented is helpful, much of it is inaccurate or silly, and sometimes it is downright harmful. Because I have long been troubled by the misinformation being disseminated to the nation's mothers and fathers, I have written *Your Kids, Their Lives: A Parent's Guide to Raising Happy, Competent, Caring Children* in an attempt to steer parents away from these false and sometimes harmful conclusions, and direct them toward ideas and techniques that have proven to be sound.

I am a psychologist, a teacher, and a parent. The psychologist and teacher part of me—30 years of teaching college-level child development and parenting courses and three college textbooks published, one specifically on parenting—led me into the heart of parenting research, in a quest to uncover the most authoritative work conducted over the past 40 years in the area of parent-child relations. The parent part of me (I have a son) was intent on understanding the complex, interrelating forces that affect the direction childrearing takes, so that I could be aware of these influences as I guided my child in a direction that would put him on a path to a successful life.

Among the experiences that influenced me most to study and write about parenting were my early career days working in a mental hospital for children and my years as a family therapist, during which I saw first hand the effects, for better or worse, of parenting. I have been especially influenced by my former students, many of whom wanted to be good parents but did not have the skills to do so. The changes they made after taking my parenting classes, and their letters of appreciation describing how well their children are doing, pushed me to share with other parents what I have learned during four decades of intense study and work.

Experts You Can Live Without

Before the 20th century, clergymen, philosophers, and medical doctors—men who didn't raise children—advised parents of their duties and goals. The ancient philosopher Aristotle argued that fathers were more important in childrens' lives than mothers; John Wesley, the 18th century theologian, proposed that wise parents should break their children's wills; and in 1894 best-selling author (before pediatrician Luther Emmett Holt) told parents to keep their children on a liquid diet until their first birthday and refrain from kissing them for fear of transmitting grave diseases.

In the mid-nineteenth century, child rearing books by Dr. Daniel Schreber were so popular in Germany they went through 40 printings and were translated into several languages. Among Dr. Schreber's views was a belief that a child's display of a temper is a sign of willfulness that must be addressed, "by stern words, threatening gestures, rapping on the bed...or if none of this helps, by appropriately mild corporal admonitions repeated persistently at brief intervals until the child quiets down or falls asleep..." This child rearing expert, whose own child was a paranoid patient in treatment with Sigmund Freud, added that in treating one's offspring this way, "you will be master of the child forever." (Swiss psychiatrist Alice Miller is convinced that this kind of parenting led Germany to unleash two wars upon the world.)

Psychologist John Watson, in his best-selling book published in 1928, told parents to treat their children as though they were young adults. He instructed, "Never hug and kiss them, never let them sit on your lap. If you must, kiss them once on the forehead when they say goodnight. Shake hands with them in the morning. Give them a pat on the head if they made an extraordinarily good job of a difficult task."

The expert of all experts, pediatrician Benjamin Spock, in his 1945 classic *Common Sense Book of Baby and Child Care*, advised parents, "a man can be a warm father and a real man at the same time.... Of course I don't mean that the father has to give as many bottles or change just as many diapers as the mother. But it's fine for him to do these things occasionally. He might make the formula on Sunday." In the 1985 edition of his book, Spock changed his mind and wrote that it is crucial to the welfare of the family that fathers do their share at home, although he didn't follow this advice when raising his own children. Aware of his own limitations, Spock cautioned, "don't be overawed by what the experts say."

A Daily Dose of Parenting Advice

It is impossible to avoid getting advice on how to raise children. My hometown newspaper, The Philadelphia Inquirer, offers parenting advice almost daily. In one sample, a fourteen-year-old girl complains, "My mom is very overprotective and I am really sick of it...she won't let me go out with any guys." An expert, billed as an "educator and consultant on early childhood and parenting education," responded with, "If you want your mom to trust you, think about what makes you trust your own friends." The answer was not only irrelevant to the inquiry, but the writer sided with the teen's mom and failed to address the issues posed by the youngster.

Two major newspapers addressed the subject of punishment within the same week. In *The Charlotte Observer*, a family psychologist advised parents to spank "as a first resort...using 'the hand only...and on the child's rear end only.'" *The Wall Street Journal* published an opinion piece that stated, "you can't raise or teach children without fear... thwacking works because it's a natural, quick and humane way to say to a child, 'behave yourself.'" If these advisors are parenting authorities, then I'm volunteering my services to the NASA space program even though I failed college physics.

In a book about homework, serialized throughout the United States, an expert advised parents to not ask "unnecessary questions, such as 'Do you need any help with your homework?'" or even, "Do you have any homework today?" The expert cautions parents, "Not only don't you offer help, you don't rush to the child's rescue if you hear him pounding his desk in frustration. Remember the value of things learned 'the hard way.'" The author relents somewhat when he suggests that if, for some strange reason, parents are asked for help by their children, the help should be limited to clarifying directions, giving examples or checking for accuracy, but only if all this parental effort takes between five and fifteen minutes, with five minutes the preferred norm. Does this "expert" really have children? It's hard to imagine any caring parent ignoring the needs of a child for help in preparing a school assignment, no matter how long it takes, particularly if the kid is pounding his head on his desk. I hardly think that the parent of any hormonally-driven, head-in-the-clouds teenager finds "Do you have any homework?" an "unnecessary question."

British psychiatrist Penelope Leach has sold millions of copies of books in the United States that say things like, "Children have always managed with good enough parents: the parents they happened to have," completely ignoring American child maltreatment statistics. Leach also writes, "Sadly, most children live in cities, and few of them experience a close community." This is a blatantly arrogant and untrue statement, given that the inner cities are home to many ethnic groups that have strong internal ties and potent kin connections throughout the community.

Again in Philadelphia, a popular radio talk show host advised parents that buying their children cars when they become of driving age will spoil them and make them irresponsible. Whether you want to make such a purchase or not is your business, but let me inform you that there has not been a single study in psychology linking a Honda Civic to battiness. (There has been a bit of antidotal evidence that suggests suburban moms are thrilled to be free of driving back and forth to high school soccer practice once the kid gets her own car.)

So how does a parent distinguish between experts who know what they're talking about and experts who have degrees in journalism or were once caterers?

Separating Opinion From Fact

Since the 1930s, the subject of parenting has developed into a discipline, a scientific field of study rooted in serious research. Researchers in psychology, sociology, and anthropology, relying on detailed observations, long-term studies, experiments, cross-cultural comparisons, and other techniques that make up scientific inquiry, have amassed an enormous amount of information related to the physical and emotional health and welfare of children. As a result, they have shown that parenting is a far more complex undertaking than most "authorities" on the subject would have parents believe. Because children's physical and psychological needs differ as they grow and develop, and the context of their lives and that of their parents continually changes, sometimes quite abruptly, no one method of parenting works for all children all the time. In other words, there is no one-size-fits-all way to raise children because there is no one-size-fits- all child. As noted child psychologist Jerome Kagen has pointed out, "Children do not require any specific actions from adults to develop optimally. There is no good evidence that children must have a certain amount or schedule of cuddling, kissing, spanking, holding, or deprivation of privileges in order to become gratified and productive adults. The child does have some psychological needs, but there is no fixed list of parental behaviors that can be counted on to fill those requirements. The psychological needs of children vary with age and the context of their growth."

What does this mean for you as a parent? How can you raise children in a way that makes them happy, competent and caring human beings if there are no written-in-stone rules by which to bring them up?

Guidelines

Although no one can guarantee you this or that kind of child if you follow a specific method or technique of parenting, there are things you can do that will help your children get on the path to successful lives, and there are certainly attitudes and strategies that hinder their optimal development. In this book I have laid out, as best I can, what these differences are.

As a parent you must face that unless you keep your children locked in the house, without access to schools, friends, or the media, there will be powerful influences other than you on their thinking and behavior, many of these forces positive and some of them destructive. The best you can do is to provide your children with the kind of experiences, particularly at home, that are likely to move them in a direction that leads them to happy, competent and caring lives, and turns them away from the forces in society that work against their best interests.

The Reward

Parenting is for posterity. One's grandchildren, and all the generations to come in a family, are affected by the kind of relationship parents build with their children. Therefore, it is important that the information and answers provided to parents be reliable. The world has changed drastically since World War II, particularly in areas of family life and childrearing. Only by knowing what is real and true about children and the context of their lives will a mother or father be able to effectively raise them.

The reward for you in encouraging and providing a life for your children that leads them to happiness, self-reliance and concern for others is a sincere and loving relationship with them, one that brings you a sense of satisfaction and feelings of joy throughout your own lifetime.

For reading ease, I have interchanged "he" and "she" and "him" and "her" throughout the book when discussing children, except where it was necessary to include both genders.

Do everything right, all the time, and the child will prosper. It's as simple as that, except for fate, luck, heredity, chance, the astrological sign under which the child was born, his order of birth, his first encounter with evil, the girl who jilts him in spite of his excellent qualities, the war that is being fought when he is a young man, the drugs he may try once or too many times, the friends he makes, how he scores on tests, how well he endures kidding about his shortcomings, how ambitious he becomes, how far he falls behind, circumstantial evidence, ironic perspective, danger when it is least expected, difficulty in triumphing over circumstances, people with hidden agendas, and animals with rabies.

Ann Beattie
Picturing Will

Chapter One
RESTLESS GHOSTS

That I be not a restless ghost
Who haunts your footsteps as they pass
Beyond the point where you have left
Me standing in the newsprung grass,

You must be free to take a path
Whose end I feel no need to know,
No irking fever to be sure
You went where I would have you go,

Those who would fence the future in
Between two walls of well-laid stones
But lay a ghost walk for themselves,
A dreary walk for dusty bones.

So you can go without regret
Away from this familiar land,
Leaving your kiss upon my hair
And all the future in your hands.

Margaret Mead
Blackberry Winter

When noted anthropologist Margaret Mead was 37 she gave birth to her only child, Catherine. Determined that her daughter become a happy, competent and caring adult, Margaret rejected many of the principles and practices of child rearing favored by American pediatricians and parents before the 1950s. She turned instead to her studies of the many cultures she had visited. She looked at the beliefs, discipline practices and child rearing results of parents in tribes throughout the world and adopted the parts of these societies that she thought would best help Catherine enjoy her childhood and become a well-functioning grownup. "I would have to work hard," she said, "not to overprotect my child, but to ensure my child's freedom to find its own way of taking hold of life and becoming a person."

This is the goal of parenting: *to raise children who can take hold of life and become their own persons.* We bring children into the world and are responsible for their care and well-being, but in the end these children must create lives that will bring them pleasure and satisfaction. They must go into the world prepared to live without us if need be, capable of building lives for themselves filled with good work, good relationships and the capacity to care about others and be an asset to their communities.

Unfortunately, many parents are failing to raise happy, competent and caring children, some because they love so much they can't let go, others because they don't care enough, and many who try their very best but simply don't have the skills needed to accomplish their goals. Here are some disturbing statistics:

• Up to 2.5 percent of children and up to 8.3 percent of adolescents in the United States suffer from depression. The rate of depression among adolescents is similar to that of depression in adults, and may be as high as one in eight. Two-thirds of children with mental health problems do not get the help they need.

• Every day, between 1.3 million and 2.8 million runaway and homeless youth live on the streets of America. One out of every seven children will run away from home before the age of 18.

17

• There are 3 million reports of child abuse or neglect in America each year. Three children die every day due to abuse or neglect. 13 percent of violence in society can be linked to earlier child maltreatment.

• An estimated one in five teenagers are current alcohol drinkers and 1 in 13 teenagers are binge alcohol drinkers.

• An estimated 1.1 million children ages 12–17 meet the diagnostic criteria for dependence on illicit drugs.

• The United States has the highest teen pregnancy rate of any developed country. By age 18, one in four young women will become pregnant. This is twice as high as England, France, and Canada; three times as high as Sweden; and four times as high as the Netherlands.

• Suicide is the third leading cause of death in 15 to 24 year olds. The rate has tripled since 1960. It is the fourth leading cause of death for children between the ages of 10 and 14.

• Homicide is the second leading cause of death for persons 15–24 years of age and is the leading cause of death for African-American and Hispanic youths in this age-group.

• More than 2 million Americans are in prison, an astonishing 715 per 100,000 citizens, the highest rate among the Western nations. More than a third of women in the nation's prisons and jails reported abuse as children, compared with 12 percent to 17 percent for women in the general population. About 14 percent of male inmates reported abuse as children, compared with 5 percent to 8 percent of men in the general population.

• It is estimated that one in every four children in the United States (28 million) is living in a household with an alcoholic adult.

It is not difficult to see the results of good parenting; happy children are contented and cheerful. Pleased with their lives, they are open and optimistic as they face each day. Their joyousness makes them pleasant to be around. Competent children have skills. They are masterful when it comes to learning necessary tasks such as speaking and reading, and they show competence in things they find enjoyable, be it building Web sites on their computers, fishing, playing the violin, cooking, shooting hoops or doing the hula dance. Children who are caring show concern for others. They are thoughtful and kind and conduct their lives with dignity and grace.

As a parent you must construct a solid foundation for your children, one built on your ability to learn and change as your children grow. You do not want to be a restless ghost blocking your children's path, but rather the person who gives them the tools they need to create happy, competent and caring lives—and then turn them loose to live them.

President Harry Truman, when asked to reveal his secret of parenting success said, "I have found the best way to give advice to your children is to find out what they want and then advise them to do it." As it turned out, his daughter Margaret did quite well by this method. She grew into an intelligent and talented young woman.

Chapter Two
BEING AND DOING

I remember riding in the backseat of my father's car and thinking I was really safe. He would take me to school and I used to play this game with him where instead of sitting in the front, I would ride in the backseat and pretend he was chauffeuring me to school. He could truly protect me then. If my parents were home, I was safe, and things didn't happen. As long as my parents were home, everything was all right.

Gilda Radner
It's Always Something

Until he was eight years old, World War II general Douglas MacArthur's mother, Pinky, dressed him in skirts and curled his hair. When he went off to West Point Military Academy as a young man, Pinky accompanied him to the school. She moved into a nearby hotel from where she could see the light in her son's dormitory room and determine if he was studying enough.

In *The Measure of Our Success*, child welfare activist Marian Wright Edelman fondly recalls her childhood as the daughter of a Baptist minister. "I went everywhere with my parents and was under the watchful eye of members of the congregation and community who were my extended parents. They kept me when my parents went out of town, they reported on and chided me when I strayed from the straight and narrow of community expectations, and they basked in and supported my achievements when I did well."

"She was just a fact of life when I was growing up," feminist writer Gloria Steinem has said of her mother, Ruth. "Someone to be worried about and cared for; an invalid who lay in bed with eyes closed and lips moving in occasional response to voices only she could hear; a woman to whom I brought an endless stream of toast and coffee, bologna sandwiches and dime pies, in a child's version of what meals should be."

Men and women become parents because of choice or chance, and they raise their children in many different ways, depending on family background, ethnicity, economic circumstances, regionality, religious orientation, socioeconomic class and the times they live in. But whether you are a member of the Inuit tribe living in Alaska or a resident of Greenwich Village in New York, your ultimate goal is to nurture, guide and protect your children in a way that takes them from immature childhood into contented, responsible and productive adulthood.

Life's Greatest Challenge

The word *parent* can be found in any dictionary, listed as a noun. From its Latin root *pario*, the word means "live-giver". The American College Dictionary suggests that a parent is a mother or a father, or more scientifically, any organism that produces or generates another. In other words, to become a parent is an easy thing: you need only to produce a child. *Parenting* is another story. This word implies action and performance. Just as there is a difference between *rain* and *raining*, so do the terms parent and parenting show the distinction between *being* something and *doing* something. As a parent you have an enormous number of responsibilities in regard to your children. So great is the obligation that it is a

21

wonder that any one person, or two working together, can manage it all.

Here are the primary responsibilities of parents, made all the more difficult because most parents are also working, managing a household, paying bills, and doing the many chores that make life run smoothly.

• On a practical level you must provide healthy food and safe shelter for your children.

• You must see that your children have proper medical and dental checkups and treatment.

• You must get your children where they have to go on a daily basis, be it school, ballet class, doctor's appointments or to a friend's house.

• You must help your children grow and develop in age-appropriate ways. Five-year-olds must learn to read, school-age children have to develop friendships, and adolescents must be encouraged toward independence. It is not appropriate for fourteen-year-olds to be pregnant or eight-year-olds to babysit younger siblings.

• It is important to teach your children practical, age-appropriate life skills such as brushing their teeth, tidying their room, making a meal or balancing a checkbook.

• Since your children must eventually go out into the world prepared to care for themselves and be self-sufficient economically, you must provide educational experiences that will help them grow intellectually and acquire competencies in areas typical to their lives.

This can entail reading to them, going to museums, listening to music, taking them fishing, teaching them to use tools, and other forms of stimulation.

• You must instill standards of social behavior that will enable your children to be respectful of others and to live in peace with the people they come in contact with.

• You have to teach your children to communicate effectively and solve problems in rational ways.

• You must provide opportunities that will enable your children to reach their full creative potential. This means also helping them to grow and meet new challenges with confidence.

• It is essential that you make your children feel loved and valued. They must be instilled with the confidence they need to lead successful lives.

• You must be understanding and supportive of your children when they go through difficult times. No one gets through life without making mistakes or confronting hardships. You are there to help your children regain their balance when they are off course.

• You must provide experiences that enable your children to enjoy life, and give them a sense of joy and happiness from being alive.

In fulfilling the daunting duties of parenting you are faced with powerful societal forces working against you, including television programming, the advertising industry, the music industry, inferior school systems, family economic stresses, corporate employment policies, cultural and religious traditions, the Internet, and peer group influences.

Despite these rivals for your children's attention, you will always be the most significant influence in their lives. Given this advantage it is important that you understand the elements that go into good parenting, and based on this knowledge, do your work well. In being forearmed with the most authoritative information to date about the parenting process you will put your children on track toward their happy and productive lives.

In the final analysis, having a child changes who you are. It changes your place in the world because you are now responsible for another person's physical and psychological well-being. While the tasks you carry out are crucially important, the relationship you build with your child, the bond of affection and respect that ties you together, will most influence his or her future.

It is usually assumed in our society that people have to be trained for difficult roles. Most business firms would not turn a sales clerk loose on customers without some formal training; the armed forces would scarcely send a raw recruit into combat without extensive and intensive training; most states now require a course in driver's education before high school students can acquire a driver's license. Even dog owners often go to school to learn how to treat their pets properly. This is not true of American parents.

E.E. LeMasters and John D. DeFrain
Parents in Contemporary America

Chapter Three
GUESS WHO'S COMING FOREVER?

We had two kids by the time we'd been married three years. They were neither planned nor unplanned; they came when they came, and we were glad to have them.... I think we had a lot of happiness in those days, but we were scared a lot, too. We weren't much more than kids ourselves (as the saying goes), and being friendly helped keep the mean reds away. We took care of ourselves and the kids and each other as best we could. Tabby wore her pink uniform out to Dunkin' Donuts and called the cops when the drunks who came in for coffee got obstreperous. I washed motel sheets and kept writing one-reel horror movies.

Stephen King
On Writing

When you make a decision to become a parent you also make a decision to significantly change your life, and yet relatively few parents know what realistically to expect after the birth of a baby. It stands to reason that major adjustments must be made within a marriage or partnership once a couple adds another person to their relationship. First and foremost, emotional resources must be shared with the new arrival. Both parents must be mature enough to accept that much of the attention and concern once given to each other will now go to the baby. More space may be needed because baby stuff takes up a lot of room. Money once spent on clothes, dining out, vacations and the like must now go for diapers, babysitters and other baby-related things.

Even when there is little or no change in feelings of love for each other, marital or partnership problems arise in a significant number of families with new babies. Because of the stress (and tiredness) that comes with a newborn, many parents argue more, communicate less and became unsure about their relationship. Problems are most likely to arise if one or both parents have low self-esteem, if a mother feels the father is insensitive to how much time and energy it takes to care for a baby, if the baby has a difficult temperament, or when parents have limited financial resources available to them. Interestingly, couples that have had an especially romantic relationship before the birth of their child exhibit more problems afterward because of unrealistic expectations that their relationship would not change.

If you are unmarried and living alone after a baby arrives, the stress of managing the care of the baby is magnified because parenting must be accomplished without a partner. In such cases it is important that you build a support system of family and friends to assist when help is needed.

Sharing Thoughts

While surprisingly few parents sit down and discuss the pros and cons of having a child before one is born (a startling number of pregnancies are not planned), it is not too late after the birth to communicate thoughts and feelings in regard to this life-changing event. Here are topics that should be discussed:

• How many children can we afford without burdening ourselves? What if one of us wants more children than the other?

• Which one of us will be primarily responsible for taking care of the baby? Will one of us stay home or will help be needed on a daily basis? Who will take care of the baby if we both work?

• Are we adjusting emotionally to not getting as much attention since having a child?

• How can we make time for each other given work and childcare duties?

• Do we have enough space to live the way we want to? Do we live in the kind of neighborhood that we're satisfied to raise a child in? What are our options in this regard?

• What are our expectations and values when it comes to raising children? How do we compromise if they are different?

• Are we in agreement about methods of discipline? What are our views on freedom or setting limits?

• How much influence should our families of origin have on our decision-making in regard to child rearing?

• How can we be sure to make our home a happy one?

The Practical Side of Raising Children

A few years ago I read an article in *Money* magazine about a Michigan couple, Mary and Rick Lathers, who have twelve children, ages 17 years to 11 months. At the time the mother was a homemaker and the father worked in the auto industry. The family income was just above what the government defines as the poverty line for a family of 14. Mrs. Lathers washed five loads of clothing a day in a cellar laundry and cooked for up to four hours. The house was scarcely furnished and the cold Michigan air came through the house's poorly insulated walls and leaky windows. Fourteen people shared a single bathroom.

Historically, it was not unusual to have a lot of children—my maternal grandmother had nine daughters and six sons —but since the West moved from an agrarian to industrial and service economies, fertility rates have dropped drastically. This is because children were once economic assets and now they are generally more on the getting end of financial support than the giving. Also, women have gained power over their childbearing lives because of modern birth-control techniques, legal abortion and economic independence. The average number of children born per woman in Western countries today is less than 2, with Italy the lowest at 1.24.

Clearly there is a practical side to parenting, as perhaps the greatest challenge in most families is to decide how many children can be afforded considering the life parents want to give their children and themselves. The cost of raising a child differs from family to family, depending on a number of factors. Some expenses, such as health care, are exclusive to each child while others, like housing and transportation, are shared. Health care and transportation will cost more in urban areas than they do rural areas.

The United States government estimates that where the Lathers live, in Michigan, it costs approximately $200,000 to raise each child from birth to age 17, not includ- ing college tuition. If you live in a suburb in Massachusetts, earn $38,000–$64,000 a year, and send your children to a public college, the cost will be closer to a half million dollars for each.

A few years ago *U.S. News and World Report* conducted an in-depth analysis comparing child rearing costs across social class lines and they came up with higher figures. They calculated into their numbers the expense of wages foregone by a parent because of child rearing duties, and the cost of a college education. According to their calculations, a typical middle-income family, making a 22-year investment in one child, needs just over $1.45 million dollars. The cost rises to $2.78 million in the top-third income bracket, and $761,871 in the bottom third. The *U.S. News* report included expenses such as prenatal care, day care, medical expenses for the child, and toys. What is unsettling about these figures is that almost one-fourth of the children in the United States live in families where the annual income is less than $15,000 a year.

Adding It Up

It is up to you to figure out realistically how many children you can afford. Is one parent going to give up his or her job? Will you need childcare help? Do you want your child to have music lessons? Go to summer camp? Have her own computer? Cell phone? What if she needs a reading tutor? How much does a prom gown cost? Or braces for her teeth? Do you expect your child to work while in high school or will you give her an allowance? Is paying for college high on your list of priorities? A private college or a public one? Do you want to camp out when on family vacations or travel to exotic places?

Very few parents take the time to figure out what the cost of raising a child is (maybe it's too scary to consider), but this is an important part of family planning. Here are the things you must consider:

• Housing will be the biggest expense. This includes mortgage or rent, property taxes, maintenance and repairs and insurance, utilities, telephone, and home furnishings. Children's rooms change as they grow and this often means changing the furniture, curtains, bedspreads and the like.

• Food costs vary greatly, depending on what and where a child eats. Figure in the costs of food purchased at a supermarket or convenience store, in restaurants, and money you might spend on school lunches. Do you buy a lot of snack foods? Fruit? Vegetables? Milk or soda? How often do you get pizza delivery?

• The cost of day care or babysitting can be substantial if parents work. Once children attend school there are supplies to be purchased and, in some cases, tuition to be paid to private schools. Other childcare and educational expenses may include special lessons, tutoring, books, sporting equipment, musical instruments and craft materials.

• Children have to be transported places—to school, the doctor's office, friends' houses. Whether you drive a car or use public transportation there are costs involved. Car payments, gasoline, insurance and maintenance add up to a tidy sum. And don't forget about the car seat for the baby.

• Clothing costs vary greatly depending on where you shop, whether you make your children's clothes, or if they are given to you. While infants need diapers, sleepwear and tiny outfits, as children grow clothing costs increase, particularly when they reach adolescence.

• Hopefully you have health insurance, either paid for personally or subsidized by your employer. Children invariably need medical and dental care throughout their growing up years. Expenses not covered by insurance can be quite costly.

• There are always miscellaneous expenses when it comes to children—personal care items, gifts, and entertainment.

• Some parents plan to pay for higher education. This is a major expense that will vary depending on whether a child goes to a public or private college, stays at home or attends school in another city, gets loans or a part-time job, or has the entire expense handled by parents. Expenses include tuition, fees, room and board, books, travel expenses, allowance and incidentals.

• While it is difficult to construct the economic cost, for some parents (mostly mothers), having a child seriously influences career advancement. Many parents leave their jobs or cut their work hours when a baby arrives. Others lose or forego promotions because of child rearing duties.

Because of economics it is not unusual today for people to have one child. Despite the perception that such children are lonely and spoiled, this is not generally the case. Only children are as well adjusted as children who have siblings, they generally do well in school, and tend to have close relations with their parents.

If you feel brave enough, you might want to realistically figure out the cost of raising a child in your family on a monthly or yearly basis.

EXPENSE CATEGORY	First Child	Second Child	Third Child
Housing			
Food			
Transportation			
Clothing			
Health Care			
Entertainment/Gifts/Toys			
Extra-Curricular Activities			
College			
*Lost Wages			
MONTHLY TOTAL			

While these figures may seem overwhelming, there is help available on both a federal and state level for parents who find it difficult to make ends meet when it comes to their children. There are federal programs for infant nutrition, school lunches, health insurance, childcare, college tuition and other child-related needs. If you need assistance, contact your state's public welfare or human services department. Much of the information you need can also be found on the Internet.

Chapter Four
INVITATION TO A DANCE

In the very beginning, as when an infant is born, the garden is capable of growing a great many different kinds of plants. Thanks to a particular soil composition (genetics), the garden may be more likely to grow some plants more successfully than others. But pretty quickly, then, the "life experience" of the garden (such as the weather it endures and the amount of care it receives) begins to select which plants take root, which are cultivated, and which are ignored. As time passes, the garden will settle into a particular pattern. Eventually, it will become more and more difficult to introduce new plants because they will find it hard to compete with those already established.

Robert Ornstein
The Roots of the Self

When John Kerry was running for president of the United States he acquired a reputation for being aloof and isolated, a man who forced himself to appear friendly and socially engaged when on the campaign trail. Part of this seeming inaccessibility comes out of a childhood spent moving around the world at the whim of his career diplomat father. John attended seven schools by the time he was in the ninth grade. When he was 12, John's parents sent him to a strict Swiss boarding school, where most of his classmates were wealthy and few spoke English. He was an outsider at the school because of his style of dress and the fact that his parents provided him with little money. Years later, John said the experience of being sent to a boarding school in a foreign country at so young an age taught him to be independent. "It taught you how to get through," is how he put it. One of his sisters saw it differently. "He missed out on mothering," she said. John's relationship with his father was also strained. John's father lived with the secret of his own father's suicide, an event that may have contributed to his emotional unavailability as a parent.

Parenting is a bidirectional process whereby the actions of both a parent and a child create a relationship. Because of the unique dynamic that occurs between a parent and a child, it is impossible to treat two children in the same way since each brings his or her distinctive personality into the relationship and each parent brings his or her own temperament and experiences. There is a synchronicity to the relationship, a dance in which parent and child act in unison to create a connection. How well the dance goes depends upon many factors, not the least of which the circumstances of a parent's life and the world in which both the parent and the child live.

The Not So Blank Slate

I gave birth to my only child when I was 38 years old. I desperately wanted a girl so that I could do girly things with her: buy pretty dresses, play with dolls, shop. My daughter would wear ribbons in her hair and pink polish on her nails. Her bedroom would be gingham and lace. She would have tea parties with friends and enjoy taking walks in the park with me. It is said, "man plans and the gods laugh." Well, the gods had a good chuckle at me. I had a boy. When the initial shock wore off I asked myself, "Now what do I do?" I didn't know much about boys, let alone this one in my arms.

My fantasies aside, whether I had a boy or a girl I would have had to learn about this child, discover who he or she was. I might well have gotten a daughter who hated pink gingham and preferred rock climbing to tea parties. It turned out that my son was so different from anything that I imagined a child would be that I often felt as if I were raising an alien.

I wrote down the things I noticed about him: he stayed up all night; he loved when his father played music on the record player we had in the baby's room; he liked when I danced with him; he preferred to snuggle with the cat rather than the dog; he paid more attention to poems than to stories; he was a fussy eater and would only try a small variety of foods; he had temper tantrums and tended to overreact when stressed. As he grew, my son cared exclusively about sports despite my taking him to museums, the library, and other places designed to stimulate his intellect. From his first day at kindergarten he said, "I hate school," and never changed his mind all the way into college. He was attracted to motorcycles and dirt bikes and spent hours in a neighbor's garage climbing on and off these machines as a little boy. He liked high-risk activities such as rock climbing and jet skiing and almost never sat still for any length of time, even when he was sick.

As a result of my observations I started my son on music lessons when he was six, sent him to an adventure camp when he was a preteen, gave him gifts of sporting equipment, paid for a lot of tutors to get him through school, bought him poetry books and sports magazines to promote his reading, took him to rock concerts, and, putting my own dread aside, purchased a quality helmet for him when, as an adult he bought his first motorcycle, against my wishes.

Although I tried hard to steer my son in certain educational directions, what I didn't do was try to change who he is because I knew how harmful that would be to his development. Early on I recognized that he had come into the world pre-wired, with a tendency toward specific interests and behaviors. It was my job as a parent to understand and work within this framework. I had observed a lot of sullen teenagers over the course of my career and knew the statistics about the number of children in our society on antidepressant medications. I didn't want this for my own child and worked hard to discover what it was that he needed to be if he was to go out into the world one day as a contented and productive adult.

As a parent it is essential that you see your children for who they are, really know them—and be fine with it. To really know them means that you understand the role genetics plays in who they are, and the way life experiences in turn influence inherited patterns.

Chemical Commands

Every newborn comes into the world complete with about 25,000 genes, chemical units that carry instructions regarding characteristics and traits transmitted through parents and from previous generations. Genes do not directly cause a child to have Grandpa's blue eyes or Great-Grandma's sewing skills; rather they encode proteins, which become the structural components of cells and the enzymes that cause chemical changes in the body. It is these chemicals that make an individual prone to behaving in certain ways.

It is genes that enable hearing, genes that promote speech acquisition, genes that shape bones, genes that give hair its texture, genes that promote musical talent, and so on. Working in groups, genes produce the proteins needed to create a little boy who might grow to be 6'2" or a little girl with red, curly hair. A couple of genes get together and you could have a fine carpenter on your hands. Another group of interacting genes might give you a world-class athlete. It is because of genes that some children are prone to shyness and others aspire to be the class clown in grade school. Genes enable youngsters to learn to read, some more easily than others. They direct one child toward fear of the dark and another toward a love of rodeo riding. It is genes that significantly influence the unique and special way a child responds to the circumstances of life. Genetic differences can lead two children to respond to the same experience distinctly. If a child's brain is coded to make him highly responsive to danger, he might feel anxious at the sight of a barking dog. Another child, genetically programmed to elicit a low-level reaction to dangerous stressors, will experience less anxiety when confronted by the dog.

The Power of Personality

At one time or another you have probably observed children at a playground. Did you notice the differences in the way they react to having to wait their turn on the sliding board, and their level of activity when on the swings and seesaws, as well as their response when another child annoys them? These differences are due to *personality*, consistent patterns of behavior that are built into the brain's neural circuitry, patterns that influence the way a child thinks, feels and acts. Because of personality one of your children will remain calm and cooperative in a crowded supermarket line and another will have a temper tantrum.

To understand your child's personality, observe the following:

• What is your child's activity level? Does he tend to move around a lot or does he prefer a slower-paced existence? Is he energetic and spirited or is he somewhat passive and reflective?

• How regular is your child when it comes to eating, sleeping and elimination?

• How positive or negative in mood is your child? Does she tend to be upbeat and happy or complaining and melancholy?

• How does your child respond emotionally to new people, objects or situations? How sociable is she? Does she move toward people in positive ways or is she somewhat reserved in social situations?

• How anxious or fearful is your child when new people, objects or things confront her? Is she shy and withdrawn or does she meet new situations with openness and courage? Is she confident or worrisome? Thoughtful or impulsive?

• What is your child's frustration level? Does he get angry, irritable or fussy when things do not go his way or does he remain calm and composed when disappointed or annoyed? Does he bounce back from adversity or give up when faced with obstacles?

• What is your child's attention level? Does she stay alert and focused when doing a task or engaging in an activity or does she get distracted or sidetracked when confronted with obstacles or opportunities?

• Is your child generally agreeable or does he tend to be antagonistic? Is he appreciative and generous? Does he show kindness and warmth toward others or does he prefer to remain somewhat aloof?

•How curious and open to new experiences is your child? Is he artistic and creative or incurious and unquestioning? Bold or restrained?

• Does he tend to be organized and efficient or undirected and disorganized? Is he likely to initiate activities or wait for others to do this?

While these behavioral descriptions focus on the extremes, you will find that your children tend toward one or the other range. Unquestionably the more understanding you have of your child's inborn personality characteristics, the closer your relationship with him will be and the easier it will be to meet his needs.

...in spite of (an) avalanche of advice, of "sure" ways to mother a child, a new mother must realize that no one of them is the only answer. She must find her own way as a mother with her own special baby. Each mother and baby is an individual. As such, each pair is stuck with its own ways of interacting. The idealized suggestions of an authority may be entirely wrong for a particular mother and her child. A young mother may be better advised to chart her own course via the markers set out by her own baby.

T. Berry Brazelton

Children Mold Their Environments

Genes and their protein agents do not stand alone in determining who a child is, the behavior he exhibits, and the person he becomes. At most, personality traits are about 50 percent determined by genes. But what makes personality so important is the power it has in creating a child's life.

One of the most interesting things about children is their ability to create the world they need in order to be satisfied with their lives—if they are not hampered by parentally-imposed obstacles or environmental deprivation. This is called *niche-picking*. An active, well-coordinated son will stay after school to play basketball with friends while a shy, introverted child might hang out in his own bedroom, downloading songs on his computer. Also, rather than becoming passive recipients of parental desires, children evoke the kind of support and reinforcement from parents that "fits" their genetic predispositions. An adventuresome son, born into a quiet, reclusive family, may insist on joining the Boy Scouts and drag his father along on camp outings. A strong-willed daughter who loves to be read to can force a busy parent to put his work aside to make time for a story. A bold, adventuresome daughter will nag a parent into taking her on a roller coaster ride at an amusement park.

Genes also affect children's lives indirectly. Whether you like it or not, your behavior as a parent is influenced by your child's personality characteristics. If you have two children and one is easy going and the other difficult, you are more likely to take the easy child with you when you run out to the supermarket for a bottle of milk. A negative and complaining child can make you less patient than you want to be. You will be harsher with your moody and difficult child than with your more pleasant child.

While parents have little influence on their child's temperament, the behaviors you reward or punish strengthen or weaken innate traits. Relatives of mine had an easy, bright, charming, outgoing, funny little girl on their hands during the first few years of her life. But the father was a screamer who impatiently berated his daughter when she didn't do exactly as he wanted, and the mother was a self-absorbed, emotionally stingy woman who never took the time to listen to the child. As an adult the daughter is sullen, mean-spirited and anti-social. This turned out to be a case of "badness of fit" in regard to both parents, a misfortune for the child.

I have seen parents yelling at their physically agile children to "get down from there." They warn "you're going to fall and break your neck" and other things designed to limit normal activity. An adventuresome child soon turns into a fearful couch potato because a parent, driven by his or her own anxieties, is unable to tolerate the child's natural inclinations. I am not suggesting that a parent allow a child to climb a tower wrapped in high-voltage wires, but rather in monitoring his or her activities, distinguish those that are really dangerous from those that are so only in the mind of a temperamentally fearful parent.

Clearly genes alone do not determine a child's future. A broad range of possibilities exist within genetic constraints. This means that experiences with a parent can turn a child in a direction that suits him or her or one that is at odds with who the child is. The best outcome of parenting occurs when a parent works with a child's innate temperament and helps fill the niche in positive ways.

Ultimately, parents have the responsibility of making the dance work. This can only be accomplished if they take the time to understand both their child and themselves. A rather passive friend of mine recently told me he has always hated to cuddle. As a little boy his mother would chase him around the kitchen table trying to get a kiss from him. When he didn't oblige, his mother felt rejected. A coolness developed between them and it lasted until her death. My friend is still a non-cuddler; however, he now has two daughters. One of them, an easy child, likes to be hugged. The father has learned to be more physical and affectionate because this is what his daughter needs. The second child, somewhat aloof, resists being fussed over or comforted when she's distressed. The father nurtures her by playing card games, going bowling, and doing other things this daughter likes.

Dance Lessons

The coordinated give-and-take, the social dance by which the behavior of children and their parents are synchronized, begins at birth, and it is an unfortunate newborn who finds himself or herself out of step with a mother or father. In a worst-case scenario, many years ago I worked in a mental hospital for children where I had a teenager in my charge who was chunky in build, slow moving, and shy. The boy's father had been a football star at Penn State and he simply could not tolerate the son he had produced. The father continually ridiculed his uncoordinated child for not being able to catch a ball. His favorite taunt was "you throw like a girl." One day the son put on a dress and lipstick to get revenge on his father. The outcome of this bidirectional relationship, obviously, was disastrous. What the father was unable to see or encourage was the boy's interest in nature and gardening.

He had a "green thumb" and managed to keep the plants in the hospital looking spry and healthy.

As a parent you can't do much about your children's innate tendencies but you can help create the world they need in order to be contented, caring and productive people. A high-energy child has to have something to do other than jump on the furniture and chase the dog around the house. You might have to find a playgroup in your area, or start one yourself. An artistic child requires materials with which to create. A negative, moody child needs a calm and patient parent, one who can point out the pleasant things in life.

In recognizing the interacting forces of genes and the environment, you will be better able to get in sync with your child. The dance will go especially well if you honor your child's uniqueness, appreciate his special characteristics, and help to make the most of his individuality.

Chapter Five

BALANCING ACT

*It is the responsibility of every adult...to make sure
that children hear what we have learned from the
lessons of life and to hear over and over that we love
them and that they are not alone.*

Marian Wright Edelman
The Measure of Our Success

When he was a 17-year-old high school junior, acclaimed
director Steven Spielberg released his first film, *Firelight*, a
story about supernatural intruders. To make *Firelight*, Steven
talked a Phoenix hospital into lending him a room and some
oxygen equipment. This work, financed by Steven's father
Arnold, cost $600 to produce and made back its investment
the first night after release. On opening night at a local
theater Arnold played the soundtrack for the movie while
Steven's mother, Leah, climbed a ladder to post the movie's
title on the theater's marquee.

As parents, the Spielbergs were endlessly tolerant of
their son's activities. They placed few limits on him, at one
point allowing him to share his bedroom with an uncaged
lizard and free-flying parakeets. Steven often cut school, choosing to spend his days playing with his father's 8mm camera
instead of sitting in a classroom learning to read. He tortured
his three sisters emotionally and was considered the terror of
the neighborhood as a youngster. Except for Leah's piano, the
living room of the Spielberg house was mostly empty so that
Steven could have room for his filming. "Nobody ever said no
to Steven," Leah has said. "He always gets what he wants,
anyway, so the name of the game is to save your strength and

44

say yes early." (Quoted in McBride, 1997)

In essence, parenting is a high-wire act, a delicate balance between *responsiveness* and *demandedness*. On one hand parents must provide their children with what they need in order to thrive physically, intellectually and emotionally. In return for this care and consideration parents understandably have expectations of their children with regard to maturity, responsibility and specific behaviors. In the Spielberg family it appears that the balance was sharply tipped in Steven's direction and, had he not been a genius, his future would probably not have been as sparkling.

The two dimensions of parenting—responsiveness and demandedness—have been studied at length by developmental psychologist Diane Baumrind and others, who have shown how these elements come together to create specific styles of parenting, each with its own characteristics, goals, and outcomes.

The Person of the Parent

How responsive and demanding you are as a parent (your basic style) depends on your own needs and wants, as well as your developmental history, family background, and life experiences. You have to be all right with yourself, content in who you are as a person, and satisfied with your life in order to be truly present in a relationship with your children. It is difficult to participate in a productive way if you are not really "there." Leah Spielberg had given up a promising musical career to raise her four children and it is possible that she saw herself and her unfilled promise in Steven and therefore allowed him to live the life he wanted almost from birth.

Clearly there are things in life that hinder full participation in parenting—job dissatisfaction, an illness in the family, marital problems, unresolved psychiatric issues, and family stress—all issues that must be addressed if a parent is to do his or her best.

The stress level in the family also influences how present a person is as a parent. Stress comes from many quarters. An acquaintance of mine is caring for a mother with Alzheimer's while trying to raise two children. One of my former students lives with in-laws she can't stand. Another of my students lives with his three children and a wife who has a drug problem.

Children can be denied opportunities for growth because of parental self-absorption, detachment, and a lack of empathy, generally called *narcissism*. Narcissistic parents exhibit an exaggerated need for reassurance and an excessive concern with external appearance over internal substance. They put their own needs and wants above those of their children.

One of the tasks of parenting is to create as stress-free an environment as possible for your children, which means working toward eliminating the problematic aspects of family life. This may mean obtaining psychiatric help for an emotionally disturbed parent, obtaining more education so that a better job can be achieved, going for marital counseling, or enlisting help for a physically ill family member.

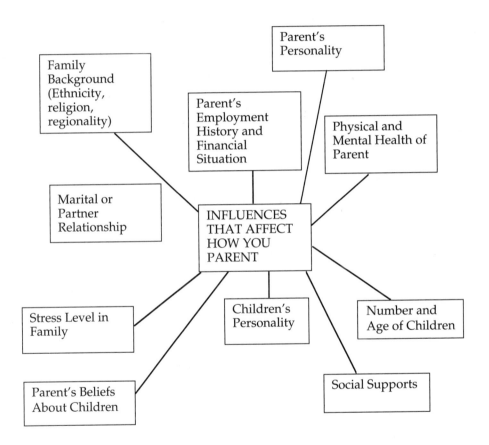

The Self-Aware Parent

When I became pregnant with my son I fantasized about the kind of mother I would be. I armed myself with Rachel Carson's *A Sense of Wonder* and prepared for long walks in the woods. My son and I would go on weekend outings—to the zoo, to the circus and to amusement parks. Truth be told, I hate the woods and never once hiked before my son was born. Acrobatics bore me. I once went to an amusement park as a child and never had the desire to return. And a stroll around a zoo seems to me to be no more than a walk in the woods accompanied by lions and tigers. At some point I had to face that I could not be the kind of mother I imagined. Like it or not my son was going to have to deal with the authentic me, the mother whose primary interests have always been her work, movies, dining out with friends, and reading non-fiction late into the night.

You come to parenting from your own special place in the world and the more aware and accepting of that place you are the more genuine you can be in your relationship with your children. Your kids won't die if you don't want to go on class trips, make gourmet meals or carve pumpkins. But they will know you are not being real if you are watching football games with them on Sunday but hate it. This doesn't mean that you can't find a compromise between who you are and what your children want. I was fortunate in that my husband enjoyed the things I aspired to do as a parent and I gladly waved him and my son off on Saturdays as they headed to places I hoped never to see again in my lifetime. You can buy brownies in the supermarket for the school bake sale if you are not inclined to make them yourself. There is no rule that says you have to attend every single soccer game or ballet rehearsal if you have pressing business elsewhere.

You can attend as many as possible and enlist a relative or friend to view others. And if there is no audience on occasion, so be it. (Leah Spielberg spent most of her days playing the piano, soaking in the sun, and playing Scrabble and cards with friends, and Steven adored her.)

As a parent you need a degree of self-awareness; that is, a realistic sense of your strengths and weaknesses and the ability to recognize your feelings and desires. It is helpful to understand what parenting means to you so that you develop clear goals concerning the outcome of your efforts. It is self-awareness that enables you to choose which way you will act in any given situation and it is this same sense of self that allows you the flexibility to change direction when you feel you have made a mistake. Self-awareness helps you communicate better with others because it makes your intentions, goals and desires in life clear. So how do you, as a parent, become self-aware? One way is to ask yourself questions and answer them honestly. Here are a few questions to ask yourself:

- What kind of people do I like to be around? Outgoing? Sports-minded? Funny? Intellectual? Religious? Liberal? Adventuresome? Creative?

- What kind of activities do I like to do? What gives me the greatest pleasure? What scares me the most in life?

- Do I have close friends? What do I like about them?

- Do I like children in general? Or do I only like my own children?

- How do I feel about my marriage or significant relationship?

49

- Do I like my job? Would I do something different if I could?

- Do I work on my relationships? Am I a good friend? Am I a generous person?

- What tone of voice do I use when speaking to others? Am I a good listener? Do I respond to what people say to me?

- How do I feel about my family of origin? Did I have a happy childhood? Do I want to parent the same way my parents did?

- What makes me upset? What do I do when I am angry or frustrated? Is my behavior mature and decent when I feel this way?

- Am I a generally happy person? What makes me grouchy?

- What are my views about money? Do I feel I have enough to live the way I want to? How generous am I?

- What makes me feel guilty? Is my guilt reasonable?

- How do I feel about being a parent? What do I like most about parenting? Is there anything I dislike?

The point of looking inward is to accept responsibility for who you are. Self-awareness enables you to build better interpersonal relationships and become kinder. It is through self-awareness that you grow—as a person and as a parent.

The Giving and the Taking

I recently paid my respects to an acquaintance whose mother had died. The woman introduced me to her family, who were sitting at the dining room table eating dinner. Her eight-year-old granddaughter was among the diners. The child absent-mindedly pushed a piece of roast beef around her plate. The girl's mother yelled from across the table, "Stop that this minute." When the child continued this behavior the mother pointed a finger at her and said, "You better not make me get up and come over there or you'll be sorry." The little girl looked up and said, "I don't want to eat with you grownups any more."

As mentioned, parents take a particular approach when it comes to interacting with their children and motivating them in certain directions. It is a parent's style of relating to his or her children that creates an emotional climate that enables parental values to be internalized by their children, accepted as a part of who they are. How strict, affectionate, warm, punitive, controlling, hostile, empathetic, accepting or rejecting a parent is are forces that pull a child into a positive emotional relationship with a parent or push him away.

Lord and Master

I suspect my acquaintance's daughter is an *authoritarian* parent, one who is highly demanding but not very responsive. Authoritarian parents value obedience and compliance in their children. They prefer to raise their children in a well-ordered, structured environment in which there is little or no room for debate or individual differences. These parents are generally harsh and critical and they attempt to control their children's behavior by threats and punishments. They often use guilt, shame and the withdrawl of love to gain psychological control of their children.

What is so interesting about the authoritarian parent is the unlikelihood of them getting what they want. Their daughters tend to be needy and dependent and their boys are often rebellious and aggressive. In other words, the girls become passive to the point of relying on controls from others, and the boys fight back against controls. In neither case do the children internalize parental goals, rather their behavior is tied to the consequences of the outside world. In some cases authoritarian parenting also leads girls to become aggressive.

The children of authoritarian parents tend to have lower self-esteem than their classmates, higher levels of depression, and poorer social skills. They may be anxious, withdrawn, irritable, moody and unhappy. Fear of punishment may make them behave as a parent wants when the parent is around but it doesn't enable them to internalize rules in a way that gives them self-control when away from that parent. Because they have been given so little control of their lives, these children have difficulty resolving conflicts.

The Freedom to Be and Not Be

Some parents tend to be *permissive* and indulgent in style, high in responsiveness and low in demandedness. While permissive parents are warm, accepting and encouraging, they have few expectations of their children and provide little structure by which their children can excel. Limits are not set and rules are not clearly communicated or enforced. Some permissive indulgent parents believe this kind of freedom leads to creativity; others want to be loved; and some are simply too tired to provide the structure their children need.

The children of permissive, indulgent parents often become self-centered, impulsive and lacking in self-control. They have difficulty respecting the opinions and rights of others. Interestingly, these children do less well in school than many of their classmates but they tend to have higher self-esteem and lower rates of depression. They are generally friendlier and more sociable then other children their age, however, they sometimes exhibit inappropriate behavior but take no responsibility for their actions. A lack of guidance often leads them to be disorganized and ineffective in their pursuits.

A unique group of parents are both permissive and neglectful, in that they are low in responsiveness but have few expectations of their children. These uninvolved parents show little interest in their children's development, and they don't spend much time with their youngsters. These children have difficulty developing the skills they need to live successful lives, and their lack of trust interferes with them having good social relationships.

Firmness, Love and Respect

The research on parenting styles favors *authoritative* or democratic parents, those who tend to be warm, responsive and somewhat demanding. These parents guide their children by firmness, cooperativeness and encouragement. They set clear limits and standards of conduct but rules are openly discussed and decided upon in a democratic way. Children are not expected to be obedient soldiers, rather, they are free to discuss judgments, values and goals with their parents. Autonomy and self-direction are considered important traits by authoritative parents. While both author-itarian and authoritative parents are high in behavioral control, democratic parents do not use shame, guilt and the withdrawal of love to gain psychological domination over their children.

The children of authoritative parents are likely to be self-disciplined and socially responsible as well as achievement-oriented and intellectually curious. They are friendly toward peers and get along well with adults. The children of authoritative parents are able to follow rules while acting independently.

The Dimensions of Parenting:

RESPONSIVENESS AND DEMANDEDNESS

Demanding But Not Responsive

The Authoritarian Parent
"My way or the highway."

Responsive But Not Demanding

The Permissive Indulgent Parent
"Whatever makes you happy."

Responsive and Demanding

Authoritative or Democratic Parent

"Let's talk about this."

Not Responsive and Not Demanding

The Permissive Neglectful Parent
"Don't bother me."

Finding Your Style

In the course of raising children you have to be aware of how you balance responsiveness and demandedness. Answer these questions and you will figure this out.

- Do you give in to your children because you can't stand it when they are upset with you?

- When you make a rule do you stick to it no matter what the circumstances? Are you able to compromise the rule when it is reasonable to do so?

- Do you feel powerless when dealing with your children? Can they overwhelm you with their demands?

- Do your children have a clear meal time and bed time?

- Do your children borrow things from you without asking? Do they put these things back after using them?

- Do you get angry and punish your children so harshly that you must reverse yourself within a short time?

- Do your children have household responsibilities? Do they volunteer to help you when they see you are in need?

- Do you express your love to your children? How often?

- Do you have family discussions during which everyone is allowed to express his or her views without being criticized or ridiculed?

- What tone of voice do you use when making a request of your children? Are you bossy? Respectful?

- Do you try to make your children feel guilty when they don't do as you say? Do you stop speaking to them when you are angry?

- Can you say "no" to your child and stick to it?

- Do you give in to whining, complaining or nagging on the part of your child?

Variations on a Theme

It is a rare parent who can live up to an ideal of parenting all the time because so many factors, including the number of children in a family, household finances, experience with children, the developmental level of children and the circumstances of a parent's life at a particular time influence the kind of parent a person is or becomes. I try hard to be an authoritative parent but I know that when I'm overworked and tired I tend to be permissive indulgent, and when this permissiveness gets out of hand, I turn authoritarian. The very best parent can become neglectful if a serious problem arises in the family and diverts attention away from the children. It is easier to be a democratic parent to an "easy" child than it is to a "difficult" child. In fact, a child who has difficulty with self-control and adjustment to change can force a more authoritarian attitude upon parents even if they want to be democratic. Parents are human and as such they have upper and lower limits of tolerance with regard to their children's behavior. As a child pushes the upper limits, parents often use increasing authoritarian methods of control.

When all is said and done what children most need from their parents to become caring, productive and psychologically healthy people are the interrelated forces of warmth and moderate control. They must feel that their parents have respect for them and their ideas, and that any problems they have can be talked about honestly and openly. Children need rules and limits but they also must understand the meaning and reason for these regulations so that their behavior will be self-regulated rather than imposed from outside and built upon fear. Most of all they must know that when they do well they will be acknowledged and appreciated for their efforts.

Chapter Six
PARENTS AS SOOTHSAYERS

Staring into the case of jewelry on the second floor of Tiffany, Elizabeth picks out her college graduation present: a necklace, a tiny silver bean linked to a thick silver chain. We go outside, on a cool and sunny spring day, and walk arm in arm west on 57th Street, the burnished necklace bright beneath her jet-black hair. I think about the ordinary miracle of rearing my only daughter to adulthood... "I used to think you had an answer for everything," my daughter says wistfully. "You can't help me anymore." Why did I imagine I could make life easy for my own child?

Francine Cournos
City of One: A Memoir

One night, when my son was sixteen, he did not come home by his 11 P.M. curfew. I called his cell phone and he didn't answer. At 11:15 I was so worried I couldn't sit still. By 11:20 I had my son dead in a ditch, his new driver's license lying beside him. Ten minutes later I was sure he had been kidnapped by carjackers. At 11:40, just as I considered calling the police, my son walked in the door. He had been to a party and lost track of the time. He hadn't taken his cell phone with him. The point of this story is to illustrate how easy it is to engage in distorted thinking when it comes to our children. The truth is, I hadn't a clue why my son wasn't home on time but this didn't keep me from conjuring up awful scenarios with no information to back up my wayward thoughts. In other words, my emotional state was a function of my own internal being and my thoughts had little to do with the reality of the situation.

Because parents differ in their beliefs about children, the same behavior in the same circumstances can lead to quite different reactions. One mother attributes a child's crying as a signal that he needs to be picked up and held, another believes the child is acting "spoiled," a third hears a hungry baby. A failed grade in a math exam can be seen as "she doesn't study enough" or "she needs extra help with the subject." A two-year-old bangs a silver spoon against a table and one father thinks the child is being "bad" while another sees it as normal behavior and gives the boy a plastic spoon instead of the silver one. In general, parents who are optimistic about life see their children's actions in a more positive light than depressed or pessimistic parents.

Myths Not To Live By

Every parent has pre-birth expectations of what their child will be like and how the experience as a mother or father will go. Think of the things you anticipated when you found out you were going to have a baby. You probably tried to imagine what he or she would look like. You thought of the fun you would have when you took your child camping, or hunting, or to art museums, or to wherever it is that you love to go. Perhaps you had fantasies about your child's future career. He'll be a fireman, like his father. She'll be a teacher, or a pianist, or perhaps both, a piano teacher. While children sometimes meet parental desires, often they do not. If your notions about parenting are not realistic, you and your child could be in for much unhappiness. There are a number of myths about parenting that, if accepted as fact, will keep you from getting the most out of your parenting experience.

Do you believe that parenting will be a lot of fun? While certainly there are fun times, the truth is, parenting is more hard work than it is entertaining. It is a daily grind of seeing that your children are well fed and clean. It is doctor appointments, help with homework, and parent-teacher nights after a grueling day at work. The fun times are intermittent. You catch a bit of amusement here and there in the course of the day and learn to savor those moments.

Do you expect children to be cute and sweet little additions to your life? Certainly they are often adorable and charming but they can also be selfish, destructive, annoying, stubborn and other things that challenge the best of parents.

Are you convinced that if you are an involved and loving parent you will raise "good" children? The truth is, you are not the only influence in your children's lives. There are powerful forces in society working both for and against you throughout your parenting years. The schools your children attend, the friends they make, the television shows they watch, the music they listen to, the advertisements they are exposed to, each has its own value system and agenda. Despite your best efforts, sometimes your children will have problems or get into a bit of trouble. Once you realize this you will be less defensive and self-blaming when painful times come, and better able to help your children through the difficulty.

Do you think that by being a good and loving parent you can manage any child? Well, temperamental differences make some children quite difficult to raise. While one youngster may be calm and agreeable in personality, another can be cranky, rigid and unable to adapt to change.

Do you expect your children to appreciate the hard work and sacrifices you make on their behalf? Sometimes they do but often children do not realize what their parents have done for them until they have their own children.

Is it enough to simply love your children? Love certainly goes a long way but unfortunately it is not enough. Raising children also requires that parents have knowledge about children, specific skills, energy and patience.

When all is said and done, parenting is both a science and an art. There is enough authoritative information available to help you make decisions and problem-solve about your child rearing concerns. The art comes in when you become so accomplished that it is second nature to you to raise your children in a way that ensures them happiness and success in their lives.

Magical Significance

Your emotional response to your children often depends on what you wish to think, which means you have more control of your reactions than you realize. Quite often the problems that arise between parents and their children are the result of a parent's distorted, inaccurate, illogical, unrealistic or irrational view.

Parents get angry with their children over a spilled glass of milk, a fight between siblings, or a teenager's mess of a room. They are giving relatively minor things more significance than they warrant. Children knock over milk glasses from time to time but not very often considering how physically active they are, siblings fight because they have mutually exclusive interests; and while the rooms of adolescents may be smelly, they are not usually health hazards. While anger may be appropriate if a child intentionally and unnecessarily acts in a harmful way, most of the things that infuriate parents do not warrant such strong emotion. When a parent behaves angrily it is usually because he or she is frightened, frustrated or just plain hostile.

> *If you can be patient in one moment of anger you will escape 100 years of sorrow.*
>
> Zen Proverb

Trailing Behind

The hardest part of parenting is to face that, just as you get a handle on what is going on with your child, the child changes, as does the circumstances of her life—and yours. She has moved on while you are running to catch up.

Consider the first two years of your baby's life. Year one consists of feeding her, changing her diapers, hugging and kissing her and basically orienting life around her needs. At about 18 months of age, your baby, through her behavior, says, "Thanks for everything. I enjoyed what you've done for me. Now back off! I have places to go and things to see. I've got to get my own life going." This can be pretty startling to any parent who has been used to having a dependent baby. It can take a bit of time to adjust to the changes of toddlerhood, but adjust you must. Otherwise you will usher in what has been called the "terrible twos," which are not, in fact, terrible at all but rather an exciting new beginning for the child. This time will become terrible only if you are unable to appreciate this transition to autonomy.

Parents as Soothsayers

So what is it you should expect at each stage of a child's development? What must be known to prepare for the inevitable changes of childhood? To parent well requires staying focused on the characteristics and tasks of specific stages. You must know what is developmentally appropriate—physically, emotionally, and socially—at these points in the life cycle. Here is the basic progression:

• Infancy (birth to 18 months) is a period of intense brain growth, leading to walking, talking and socializing. During this period it is essential that parents provide good nutrition, a stimulating environment, and an emotional closeness that leads the child to feel safe and secure.

• Early childhood (18 months to age 6) is a period of dramatic physical, social and intellectual growth. It consists of the preschool and nursery school years, a period of exploration, play and the development of self-sufficiency, which lead children to become increasingly willful and independent. It is at this stage, through language development, that children learn how to think. Through language they come to understand the customs, ideas, ideals, emotions and religions of their culture.

• Middle childhood (ages 6–11) is a bridge across which children must successfully pass if they are to enter the world beyond childhood. It consists of the school-age years when the emphasis is on learning fundamental skills of reading, writing, math and other competencies of their culture. More complex thinking and reasoning abilities become evident at this stage, enabling children to become increasingly capable of logical thought, and of seeing the world from the point of view of others.

• Adolescence (ages 11 to about 20) is the period between childhood and adulthood when dramatic changes occur physically and psychologically. It is a time when children struggle with issues related to their changing bodies and emerging sexuality, as well as separation, independence and peer relationships. During this stage they must be educationally prepared for a future in which they are self-sufficient.

Crystal Balls

Some parents pride themselves on being mind readers. "I know you don't want to spend time with me," or "You knew it was your grandmother's birthday and you deliberately stayed at your friend's house instead of visiting her." Do not assume that your children are considering you when they make decisions. Children live in their own minds and worlds and what they are thinking has far less to do with their parents than parents like to admit. Consider your own thinking processes when you make forceful statements.

• Do not magnify or minimize actions or events out of proportion to what is realistic. "You'll never get into college with these grades." "That friend will bring you to ruin." "It's meant to be that you didn't make the team." If you make a bigger deal of things than is warranted, your children will avoid telling you anything. If you dismiss your children's concerns, they will see you as insensitive and uncaring. Keep things in perspective when talking to your children.

• Do not assume that your negative emotions are accurate perceptions. "I feel it in my bones that your new friend is bad news, and I'm never wrong when I sense these things." "I went through something like this when I was your age and let me tell you, it always turns out badly." While you may have an "instinct" about something, it is important to focus on the facts of a situation. What is it that you find disagreeable about your child's friend? Is it a valid enough reason to dislike this child? How relevant is your past experience to the one your child is a part of? Is old emotional baggage getting in your way?

• Do not make "right and wrong" issues out of personal desires. "You should call your grandmother today." "You ought to read more books." "You should take a bath every night." It is nice for a child to call a grandparent, and it's to a child's advantage to be a good reader. Avoid "shoulds" and "oughts." It is better to explain to children the reason for a request or a rule. "Grandma would love to hear from you today because she's feeling a little lonely. Please call her." "The better you read, the better you will do in your classes. Let's go to the library and take out some books." "You'll have more friends if you take a bath every night and are clean when you go to school."

• Do not assign negative labels to your child when his behavior is considered inappropriate. "You are really lazy." "How dumb can you be?" "You are a bad boy." Labeling a child in this way does not provoke a child to do better, rather, it may cause him to give up. Children are not "bad" or "bratty" or "stupid" or "slobs," rather they are young people who are doing or being something you don't approve of. Name-calling is a destructive technique because it goes to the heart of who a child is. How do you expect "stupid" to do better in school if he thinks of himself the way he has been labeled? "Bad" kids don't act "good" because you call them bad.

Guess what? Children make mistakes and errors in judgment. A daughter cuts her high school math class to go shopping with a friend and the school counselor calls home to say she is in danger of failing the subject. A son leaves the house and forgets to lock the door. These are not major crimes but rather actions that have to be dealt with sensibly. It is your job to help your children think about and realistically evaluate a situation that has not turned out well for them. Making mistakes are a part of everyone's life, and it is often the part that teaches us the most. Good parents accept mistakes in themselves and their children without dwelling on them or exaggerating their effect. As educator Rudolf Dreikurs notes, "We all make mistakes...Our children will maintain their courage and learn more readily if we minimize the mistakes and direct their attention toward the positive. What is to be done now that the mistake is made leads to progress forward and stimulates courage. Making a mistake is not nearly as important as what we do about it afterward."

Chapter Seven
HEARTH AND HOME

Your family is what you've got... It's your limits and your possibilities. Sometimes you'll get so far away from it you'll think you're outside its influence forever; then before you figure out what's happening, it will be right beside you, pulling the strings. Some people get crushed by their families. Others are saved by them.

Peter Collier
Downriver

Former president Bill Clinton's father died in an auto accident shortly before Bill's birth. His mother, Virginia Blythe, then moved in with her parents and turned the care of her baby over to her mother Edith, a strong-willed woman who had a terrible temper and a mean streak. When he was a year old, Virginia moved away and left her son behind. Edith ran her grandson's life with precision. She made him eat and drink at assigned times, put him to bed and woke him up on a rigid schedule, and even forced food into his mouth when she thought he should eat more. Edith focused on two aspects of Bill's education: she took him to church and taught him to read when he was two. When Bill was four-years-old Virginia remarried and, after a struggle with Edith over custody of Bill, she took the boy to live with her and her new husband, Roger Clinton. An alcoholic, gambler and wife abuser, Roger never adopted Bill, although Bill took Roger's last name as his own. Virginia loved her son but taking care of him was not a priority. She worked long hours as a nurse and when off duty relaxed by hanging out with friends, drinking, and gambling at the racetrack. Virginia turned Bill's care over to an older woman who, recognizing

Bill's keen intelligence, assured him he would make a fine minister.

Every child is born into a family of some kind and whether it is somewhat chaotic, as in Bill Clinton's case, or quiet and peaceful, it is within this setting that children first learn who they are, how the world works, and what possibilities the future holds. It is within families that children learn values, gender roles, beliefs, expectations, attitudes and social skills. It is here that they find out if they are lovable.

In the United States children are often viewed as separate beings within their families, and their behavior at any specific time is not linked to other household happenings at the same moment. Parenting advice manuals offer generic suggestions about bedwetting, temper tantrums and other problems implying that a specific parental action will change a child's behavior. But bedwetting or temper tantrums have different meanings depending upon a child's age, developmental level, life circumstances, and family dynamics. In one family the bedwetting may start at the point when parents are talking about divorce; in another, a child may have an undetected illness. Temper tantrums have myriad causes including frustration, tiredness, hunger and even the imitation of a parent's reaction when something goes wrong. To create a happy family you must understand the underlying dynamics of family life and honestly appraise whether your family is working in ways that bring you and your children together in harmony.

An Arrangement of Parts

A major objective of family life is for people to live in harmony, so that they can be helpful and supportive of each other. In a musical sense harmony refers to the pleasing arrangement of parts. This definition also applies to families, in which many different personalities must come together to create a lovely mix. While it is often difficult to reconcile the needs and wants of everyone in a family, it is a parent's responsibility to see that family life is fair and each family member feels cared for and considered.

Families come together as a system, an organized structure of interrelated relational parts. Family members connect on an emotional level so closely that a change in one person affects the behavior of the others. Think about what happens if children are enjoying themselves playing a game of Scrabble® and a parent walks in from work in a bad mood and begins hassling them for leaving dishes in the sink. Most likely the game ends. Now consider the effect of the parent walking in with a box of donuts in hand and a cheery outlook.

Much of family life consists of tasks to be done (food cooked, bills paid, snow shoveled, clothes washed, homework completed, the dog walked), daily situations to face (getting to work on time, handling a family illness), problems to be solved (deciding where to go on vacation), emotional needs to be met (comforting an upset child), and family standards to uphold (disciplining children and maintaining boundaries). This necessitates family members taking on roles, which means that they have specific tasks and responsibilities. These roles are based upon age, gender and personality characteristics or interests. It is through roles that children learn how to handle emotional feelings, the type of activities to pursue, and how to behave toward others. Historically, roles were thought to be the function of biology. Men, considered the stronger and smarter sex, had tasks such as driving tractors and managing money; women were responsible for cooking, cleaning and other household chores. Today, gender roles are interchangeable. Women fix doors, play ball with their children and invest in the stock market; men cook, do laundry quite competently and soothe crying infants.

If the Role Fits

Someone has to be in charge in a family and that someone is parents. But "in charge" does not mean running a family like tyrants. "In charge" means assigning roles with the best interests of everyone in mind. In my own family I hate to cook and my son loves to cook. He does the food shopping and cooking; I do the dishes. In my friend Lea's home, Lea does the food shopping, her mother does the cooking and Lea's husband does the dishes.

As a parent, take time to discuss the responsibilities of the adults and children in your family. Find out how they feel about the roles they have been given or adopted. Take note of who is burdened by his role, and who does not hold up an end when it comes to family responsibilities. Find out who is satisfied. If the role of a working mother in the family is also to do all of the household chores, resentment and exhaustion will result. In families where there is an insistence that a child get top grades in school, problems will arise if a child is stressed beyond his abilities. In the end, only if family members believe that their roles and responsibilities are fair and equal will there be satisfaction and peace in the home. When looking at family roles, here are some of the questions you might consider:

• Who brings in income? Who controls the money? Who decides what the family will spend money on?

• Who does the food shopping and house cleaning? Is it always the same person?

• Who feeds and walks the dog? Who takes the cat to the vet for her shots?

• Who drives grandparents to their doctor appointments? Who picks up their medications at the pharmacy?

• Who does the holiday gift shopping? Who are the gifts for?

• What expectations are placed on the children in the family? Are they realistic?

• Who do the children go to when they are upset? Who do you go to when you want to talk about a problem you are having?

• Who sees that the children's homework is completed? Which family member attends parent-teacher night at school? What is expected of a child educationally?

• Who disciplines the children in the family? Who sets the standards of behavior for family members?

• Who makes the major decisions? Who has the final word when there is a difference in opinion?

• Who sees that the major functions of family life get accomplished? Who determines if the roles of family members are appropriate? Are the gender differences fair?

• Are children expected to do more or less than is developmentally appropriate?

When the Role Doesn't Fit

In troubled families, roles are often maladaptive. One of my clients resented that her husband expected her to go alone to buy Christmas gifts for his parents, siblings, nieces and nephews because he hates to shop. Another client did not like to be put in a position of disciplining his stepson. He felt it was the boy's mother's responsibility. I've had many female students who complain that as children they had to do the dinner dishes, which took an hour, and their brothers had to take out the trash, which took five minutes.

A particularly troubling role in some families is played by the child who has become *parentified*, that is she, in subtle ways (usually through guilt), has taken on the protective and caretaking duties that are the responsibility of parents. The parentified child, out of an intense loyalty, tries to satisfy the family's practical and emotional needs. An 11-year-old girl does the family's food shopping and laundry because her parents work long hours, but these responsibilities keep her from developing the friendships that are appropriate at that age. A 16-year-old boy becomes his mother's confidant and companion because of his parents' unhappy marriage.

One of my students, Christopher, was raised with a single mother who worked two jobs. His maternal grand-mother took care of the house and cooked. When he was 15, Christopher's grandmother was diagnosed with cancer. For two years, until her death, it was his responsibility to feed and bathe his grandmother and see to all her needs. An honor student all through school, Christopher often had to stay home to care for his grandmother and he got so behind in a number of subjects that his dream of getting into an Ivy League college was crushed.

A client of mine, Rebecca, had a sister a year younger than she, and in early childhood they lived carefree lives, playing with each other and neighborhood children. When Rebecca was 10 her mother became pregnant accidentally and gave birth to a baby boy. The mother basically handed the baby over to Rebecca, who fed and diapered him and generally took care of all his needs. As a 40-year-old Rebecca stills lives with her parents and spends her weekends babysitting her sister's children. Rebecca did not attend college but she helped pay for both her sister and brother to go.

Unfortunately, a significant number of children in our society are required to sacrifice their childhood or adolescence to assume a parental role in the family, particularly when there are economic difficulties, marital conflict, divorce, substance abuse, mental illness and other problems at home. Those who are severely parentified may suffer a lifelong sense of loss, anger and resentment, guilt, disruption in identity development and conflict about leaving home.

Don't Grow Up

A childhood friend of mine was not allowed to ride a bike or skate when he was a youngster because his mother feared he would be injured if he fell. He had no chores or responsibilities at home and he generally got his way by having temper tantrums. Both his mother and an older sister continued to direct my friend's life all the way into adulthood, mostly through continual criticism of his friends, his interests and occupation, and even his appearance. As an adult my friend's misdirected anger led to two failed marriages and difficulties at work. Most of his life he has suffered from undiagnosed depression.

In contrast to the parentified child, an *infantilized* child like my friend functions at a subnormal level. This child's needs are met to such an extreme that he is incapable of doing any practical or emotional caregiving of himself or others. The parents of infantilized children keep their youngsters from carrying out age-appropriate responsibilities, making decisions for themselves and accepting the consequences of those decisions. This keeps them dependent and unable to grow up.

The most significant problem with both parentification or infantilization is the child's internalization of either role. Over-functioning can become a part of the child's character, making her feel a lifelong compulsion to take care of others and sacrifice her own well-being, if need be, to do this. This is the teenager who listens endlessly to her friends' problems, asking little for herself in the way of friendship; the young adult woman who relents to having sex with a persistent date; and the middle-aged father who works long hours but goes to every sports activity his children participate in, no matter how exhausted he is. Similarly, the under-functioning child may come to identify with her helplessness and live a life of reliance on others to take care of her and tell her what to do.

I am not suggesting that children not be loyal and helpful to their families, but it is one thing for a 14-year-old to babysit for younger siblings and quite another for her to feed and dress them daily because a parent who drinks too much cannot properly care for the children. It is important that family role assignments and responsibilities be clear, reasonable and developmentally appropriate. An eight-year-old should not babysit for a six-year-old and a 15-year-old has no business hearing about her divorced father's sex life. While parents can be "friendly" toward their children, they must understand that their children should not take on the role of peers.

Family Rules

During the 2004 presidential election campaign I had dinner at a friend's house and during the meal I brought up the subject of George Bush versus John Kerry. My friend's adult daughter told me that politics, religion and sex are not to be discussed at the dinner table. When I asked her why, she said that these subjects stir people up and the differences in opinion among family members cause people to get upset. I found this interesting because in my family, dinnertime is ripe for heated arguments about anything from should Bill Clinton have been impeached to which breed will win at the Westminster Dog Show. The feelings of the people in my family don't warrant much consideration because nobody takes the debates personally. The difference between my friend's attitude concerning speech regulation and my own illustrates the way families are governed by the rules they create.

Every family settles on regulations, sometimes stated but most of the time unstated but understood by all family members: Everyone must sit down to dinner at the same time; children "should be seen but not heard;" "there is no TV until homework is completed" are examples of family rules. There may be an unwritten rule in the family that mother controls the money and it's better to ask her for something after dinner when she's relaxed and in a good mood. Perhaps everyone knows to stay out of "Dad's chair."

There are families that do not regulate speech, even if members are yelling or cursing at each other. I know of a family that makes it clear that if one member has a falling out with someone, the rest of the family cannot have a relationship with this person. In some homes it is dictated that dishes be washed immediately after use and in other families dishes can be piled in the sink until Mom gets home from work and puts them in the dishwasher. In some families all meals are served at the kitchen table, in others children eat in the living room while watching television. There are set bedtimes in some families, and children fall asleep on the living room couch and are carried up to bed in others.

The Purpose of Rules

In laying down rules, parents must think about whether their policies lead to harmony in the family and the well-being of their children. What purpose does it serve not to allow children to express opinions? Is it to anyone's benefit if family members insult each other when upset? Is it helpful to avoid all mention of sex and birth control with your teenage children? A single parent may want his or her date to sleep over, but is this a good policy when there are children in the house?

As a parent you are responsible for making the rules. In doing so, consider the following:

• Are the rules fair to everyone in the family? Are rules for the boys different from those for the girls? Is there a good reason for this?

• Do the rules set a good example? Do they benefit the children?

• Do the rules put family members in uncomfortable positions? Do they interfere with good interpersonal relationships?

• Are the rules age appropriate? Children grow and change and the rules must change with them.

• Does one parent always have the final word about the rules? If so, what does this teach children about relationships?

• Are the rules so rigid and inflexible in your family that they do not work for the overall good of family members?

• Are the rules so lenient that the children's health and welfare suffer?

• Are you able to make rule changes in accordance with family needs and circumstances?

Encouraging Individuality

A few years ago I came across a biography of Orville and Wilbur Wright, the brothers noted for making the world's first successfully-controlled flight at Kitty Hawk, North Carolina in 1903. Born four years apart but called "inseparable as twins" by their family, both brothers dropped out of high school, never married and never left their father's house. They lived together, ate together, played together and worked together every day of their lives until Wilbur's death from typhoid fever in 1912. What is especially interesting about this relationship is that it was built upon the death of the family's real twins, Otis and Ida, who were born three years before Wilbur, and whose birthday was celebrated for over 25 years. After Wilbur's death, Orville developed the same kind of relationship with his sister Katharine, with whom he shared a birth date. When Katherine became engaged to be married at the age of 52, she was terrified of telling Orville. Once she did, Orville never spoke to her again.

Family health often rests on the degree to which family members show an interest in each other and invest themselves in family matters. At best family members fulfill appropriate role responsibilities and show warmth and concern for each other while respecting boundaries and individuality. Sometimes, as in the case of the Wrights, family members are not able to balance the desire for togetherness and the need for separateness.

Connect and Separate

As people grow and develop, they engage in a continual struggle between connectedness and separateness. A two-year-old wants to be with his mother at the dinner table but refuses everything she offers him to eat. Adolescents call home but they don't want their parents to ask too many questions about what they are doing. American culture emphasizes autonomy—rugged individualism—independence in one's thoughts and actions, but many of the people living in the United States today have been raised in cultures that promote collectivism, a togetherness that relies on family members doing what they see as best for everyone and not just themselves, often, in fact, putting the needs and wants of family members before their own.

The ability to function as both part of a group and as an individual is a tricky life task. This means balancing between individuality and autonomy, togetherness and fusion. Obviously a newborn is completely dependent on his mother for care and nurturance. Infant survival depends on emotional connectiveness with his mother and this fusion extends to the family. To some extent this emotional connection lasts a lifetime, although the strength of the connection differs from individual to individual within a family.

In a family in which members are treated as distinct individuals there is less pressure for emotional connectedness. The child comes to view his parents and siblings as individuals with differing feelings and beliefs. Acceptance and approval does not depend upon "feeling" the same as everyone else in the family.

The Collective Force

In some families the togetherness force is so strong that children cannot separate emotionally from parents. Parental anxiety becomes a family affair with the children pulled into the parents' emotional field. This is particularly true in a divorced or divorcing family when each parent turns to his or her children for support.

The degree to which families enable members to separate their own thoughts and feelings from those of others determines how healthy a family is. While the degree of differentiation varies according to ethnicity and specific families, it is difficult for children to be content if they feel they must always agree in order to be accepted and loved. When children are seen as individuals within the family they are free to express themselves honestly and make decisions based on their own needs and desires. This doesn't mean that family members who develop an emotional separateness do not care about each other. In fact, family harmony is likely to be increased because of the love and acceptance family members feel from each other despite differences. It is by helping your children become independent that you prepare them to develop relationships outside the family.

In happy families there is a warmth and closeness that comes from being together. The family is solid and unified, providing roots for its children. Family members get pleasure from spending time together. They display their love physically (through touch, and with smiles, hugs, and kisses) and verbally (by saying "I love you" or "you're a terrific kid"). They share chores and make a point of planning recreational activities that all will enjoy, whether it's a walk in the park, a card game, or a vacation to the beach. At the same time there is a deep respect for individual differences and pride in a child's quest for independence. In such families, children grow wings.

When you consider how differentiated you and your children are, think about the following:

• What is your reaction to what your children wear, the music they listen to, the friends they choose, their career choices and their opinions?

• When you feel strongly about something, how do you present your views? How do you react when your mate or children disagree with you?

• Are you able to give your children suggestions and advice without nagging, making them feel guilty or berating them to take it?

• How involved do you get in the things your children and other family members do? It is one thing to show an interest in the goings-on in the family and another to insist on being a part of every activity or decision.

• Does your family include nonfamily members in its circle? Have family members built friendships with people outside the family? Are these friends welcome in your home?

• Do you plan activities together as a family and enjoy doing them? Do these activities take into account the likes and dislikes of all family members?

• How do family members communicate their love and acceptance of each other?

Enmeshment and Disengagement in the Family

People who saw the popular 2002 film *My Big Fat Greek Wedding* laughed uproariously at the story of a family without boundaries, whose members got emotionally involved in every aspect of each other's lives, expressing their approval or disapproval of everything from career and dating choices to wedding attire and home buying. While such closeness seems appealing in a movie, in real family life this degree of oneness or enmeshment poses problems for individuals who want to live lives somewhat independently of the family.

In some families there is a sense of "all for one and one for all" so intense that parents and children are not able to see each other as individuals. In enmeshed families, members are overly involved in each other's lives. If one person is upset about something, everyone gets into the emotional act.

When there is a problem, everyone rallies to solve it, even if the problem has nothing to do with him or her. There are no distinct roles in the family and as a result there are no boundaries between family members. The enmeshment keeps family members from developing into their own persons, with feelings and thoughts different from everyone else's.

You don't have to look hard in some families to find close relatives not speaking to each other for long periods of time. While it sounds inconsistent, this kind of disengagement is sometimes built upon enmeshment. In these families the lack of individuality is so strong that when someone does break out of this smothered state he is seen as a traitor to the family. As a result there is a break in the relationship and the individualized person becomes an outcast.

The Triangle

Recently my sister became annoyed at me because I wouldn't go to my computer to order her a sweater she'd seen in a catalog (my favorite television program was on and I wasn't budging from my chair). My sister's husband called a few minutes later to tell me he thought I was being inconsiderate. This is an example of a common family dynamic—triangulation. The triangle plays an important role in a family's emotional system. During periods when anxiety is low and calmness prevails, family members engage in comfortable dialogues, pleasantly chatting about work or school or romance or whatever; however, when the stability of the family is threatened or if one or more family members becomes upset or anxious, tension is lessened when one of the parties "reaches out" and pulls another person (and sometimes two or three persons) into the conflict in an attempt to stabilize the conflicted relationship.

Emotions "overflow" to the third person, or that p
be emotionally "programmed" to initiate inv
As a result, this triangle dilutes the anxiety, the
relationships from emotionally overheating. Among parents
and their children, a triangle can occur when a mother or
father, unhappy with his or her mate's emotional distance,
becomes increasingly involved with one of the children.
While most parents make comments from time to time such
as, "Your mother is a terrible driver," or, "I wish your father
would drink less at parties," complaints relayed to a child
from one parent about the other sets up a pattern of triangulation and puts the child in an uncomfortable position.

"Mom, can I go to a sleepover
this weekend at Jennifer's?"

"Not this weekend. We have to be
up early on Sunday to go to Grandma's
for her birthday."

"OK."

A calm relationship:

"Dad, it's important that I go to Jennifer's sleepover but
Mom won't let me. All the girls will be there."

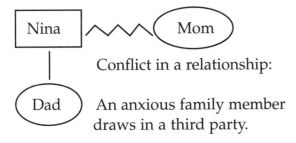

Conflict in a relationship:

An anxious family member
draws in a third party.

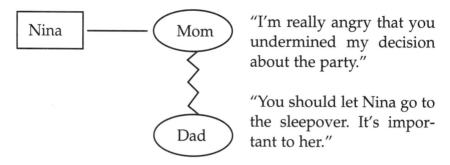

"I'm really angry that you undermined my decision about the party."

"You should let Nina go to the sleepover. It's important to her."

The conflict has shifted away from the original relationship to a new twosome.

It Started Long Ago

In thinking about your family structure and the roles, rules and interactions with your children it is important that you take a realistic view of the family you grew up in—your family of origin. All of us, on some level, remain loyal throughout life to the family that raised us. This loyalty, conscious or unconscious, is reflected in the way we feel, think and behave. Within your family of origin you internalized beliefs about relationships, especially that of parent and child. It is from your parents that you first learned how to be a parent, simply by the way they treated you, and the roles and rules they promoted.

Think about your family-of-origin's beliefs and behaviors when it came to raising children. Which of these assumptions and actions have you carried into your present relationship? Are they such that they created a happy home for you as a child?

• Did your family of origin live in harmony? Were people considerate of each other?

• What style of parenting did your parents favor? Authoritarian? Permissive? Democratic?

• How did your parents view gender roles? In what way were the boys treated differently from the girls? Were responsibilities gender bound?

• What kind of relationship did your parents have with each other? How did this impact their parenting practices? Did they see parenting the same way?

• What were your parents' beliefs about education, friendships, animals, dining out, shopping, caring for elderly relatives, work, the military, religion, money, holidays, sexuality, music and anything else you can think of?

• How were nonfamily members viewed in your family? Were nonfamily members welcome in your house?

• Were there things your family believed in or did that were harmful to satisfactory family life? Was there addiction in the family? Mental illness?

• Did your parents enjoy having children? How did they show affection?

Being objective about one's family of origin and its styles of parenting is not an easy thing, but the better you understand your past, the better you will be able to continue those aspects of your childhood that made you happy, and the more likely you will be to change those things that didn't work well for you.

It is also important that you discuss your family-of-origin's beliefs and behaviors about parenting with your mate or partner. He or she may come from an entirely different perspective. In uniting with another person and having children, two families are brought together. From these two families a new family system evolves, one that hopefully brings happiness to you and your children.

Troubled Times

There is no getting through family life without problems, and one of the most difficult is the ending of a parental relationship, by divorce or separation.

Divorce has been characterized as "one of the more demanding tasks that rational beings are expected to perform." It is difficult to imagine a more traumatic family event, other than a death, as divorce interrupts the normal developmental patterns of family life. Even when both parents agree to a divorce and they handle the separation as amicably as possible, family members feel fear, worry and concern for the future. Can the family of divorce be happy? Of course. But it takes work, patience and good behavior on the part of parents.

Divorce begins emotionally as one or both parents decide that the marital relationship is not working. Physical separation follows, bringing with it feelings of hurt and failure. The legal proceedings that redistribute assets, determine child custody rights and support payments and work out visitation add additional stress to the situation. Often families change their place of residence after a divorce, necessitating a change in friendships, neighbors, schools and other aspects of social life. The families of divorce usually have less money available to them, particularly when one parent is responsible for supporting the family. While there has been an increase in the number of fathers who retain custody of the children after a divorce, most children remain with their mothers. Many noncustodial fathers see less of their children after a divorce, as a result of their own pain and anger, and others become more attentive now that they are on their own with the children.

There are four factors that most determine the adjustment of children to a divorce or separation in the family:

• the degree of conflict experienced between the parents;

• a continued relationship with both parents after the divorce or separation;

• the kind of responsibilities given to children after the divorce or separation; and

• the degree to which children accept the reasoning behind the divorce or separation.

Children often fear that they will be abandoned as a result of a divorce or separation in the family. There are fears that the custodial parent will leave, and adults now appear less trustworthy and reliable. Reactions to and the effects of divorce or separation on family life vary according to the age of the children, personality factors, family dynamics, religious and ethnic heritage, socioeconomic status and other factors that make up the life of those going through this transition; it is not unusual for the children of divorce to become depressed or act out behaviorally for a time. They may also exhibit problems in school. At home there is sometimes a breakdown in rules and discipline as one or the other parent becomes either distracted by family problems or indulgent and permissive in an effort to compensate for the family breakup.

The Good Divorce

Much of the public debate over divorce has focused on the negative aspects of this family change; however, it must be emphasized that millions of children have lived through this family reorganization and have done quite well in life. This is accomplished when the adults in their lives handle the family breakup with maturity, sensitivity and concern for their children's adjustment.

Some conflict is inevitable in cases of divorce but parents must do their best to minimize it, as it is the hostility between parents that often damages children more than the divorce. Here are some rules to follow:

• Children do best when both parents remain actively involved in their lives. This means divorcing parents must help their children remain as close as possible to both their mother and their father, unless there is danger involved, as in the case of a parent who is a criminal or drug addict.

• Children benefit from maintaining family relationships in their life that were important and meaningful to them prior to the divorce. This usually means not only parents but also extended family members, such as grandparents and aunts and uncles on both sides of the family.

• While roles and rules may be different in the house-holds of divorced parents on major issues, such as schoolwork or rules for driving, parents should work together and agree on expectations about their children's behavior.

• Problems and disagreements between parents should be worked out privately, without pulling the children into the fray.

• Children should not be used to transfer messages between parents or carry requests for money or child support.

• Parents should refrain from sharing confidences about the divorce with their children or enlist their children's help in spying on a former partner.

• Family members must not "bad-mouth" one or the other parent to the children, no matter what the circumstances. Children find out soon enough on their own about a parent's good or bad character.

• Disagreements between divorced or separated parents must be kept civilized and peaceful. Under no circumstances should there be any violence or mistreatment by either party involved.

• Parental disputes should have limitations in terms of time and place. They should not go on and on to the point that they are the major focus of family life. Parents can decide, for example, "to talk tomorrow at a neighborhood coffee shop and come to some agreement about this issue."

Children need extra attention from their parents after a divorce, at precisely the time that parents are dealing with their own issues concerning the separation. Despite these difficulties, parents must put the best interests of the children first. To create a happy family in the midst of divorce, children need a lot of love and nurturing. While they will invariably be distressed, they will adjust well if parents maintain a cooperative and civilized partnership in raising them.

The Happy Stepparented Family

Former President Bill Clinton is a man who, while growing up, had one mother, two fathers, one half-brother and many stepsiblings, most of whom he didn't know. This makes him a lot like millions of other Americans now being raised in stepparented families.

Since about 60 percent of second marriages also end in divorce, many children in stepfamilies experience a second splitting apart of their families. Often second-time divorcees marry again, thus adding to the complications of the stepfamily.

Stepparenting is a complex phenomenon because so many variables determine its success or failure. What makes it especially hard to build a happy stepparented family is the lack of clear guidelines concerning roles, responsibilities, financial obligations and legal standing. Resolving practical issues of space and household management pale next to dealing with the emotional issues of power and loyalty, competition and resentment that often emerge when families blend. The success or failure of stepparenting is built on factors that include prior experiences of all members of the family, the sex, ages and developmental stages of the children in the blended family, the psychological issues of the parents, and the way differences between family members both within and outside the blended family are negotiated.

It Takes Time

If you are a parent in a stepparented family you must recognize that adjustment comes in stages. In the beginning, when new partners and their children come together, children often feel angry. They experience a sense of loss and sadness for the life that is now surely left behind. Family members often have hopes and expectations about the new family constellation, some of them unrealistic. Sometimes a divorced and still unmarried parent, who doesn't have child custody, feels threatened when an ex-mate brings a new partner into the parenting picture. A stepparent with obligations to two families often has difficulty negotiating time, money and affection between the two households.

A parent who wants to heal the biological family from the effects of divorce by bringing in a new partner may be disappointed when this healing doesn't occur. Stepparents who expect to be loved by their stepchildren and welcomed into the new family may feel hurt and resentment when the children see the stepparent as an intruder. Problems arise in stepparented families when the developmental stages of the children are incompatible with a particular phase in the stepfamily's history. For example, at time when a stepparent seeks more closeness and greater authority, an adolescent in the family may be pulling away due to struggles with identity, new relationships, sexuality and plans for the future, issues that have nothing to do with the stepparent.

Stepparenting Success

The success of stepparenting depends in part on the age of the children when a stepparent enters the family and the living arrangements are worked out between the custodial and noncustodial parents. In cases of shared custody or visitation agreements the transition back and forth on a scheduled basis can be stressful to a young child. The children's primary attachment will often be to their biological parent; this can make a stepparent feel left out.

Preschool-age children are most likely to bond to nurturant stepparents when there is little or no contact with a noncustodial parent. Children older than three understand the family situation better than preschool-age children and they sometimes feel torn between the adults in their lives. When there is a strong attachment between a child and her custodial parent, the addition of a stepparent can cause the child to feel a sharp loss when a parent's time and attention, once given to the child, goes to the new relationship.

To create a happy stepparented family, parents must confront family conflicts and peacefully negotiate issues, such as food preferences, the organization of household tasks, privacy needs and space requirements. The new family system must reorganize itself by clarifying the differences between two parental households while strengthening the boundaries in the stepfamily. It can take as long as three-to-five years for a stepparent to be considered less of an outsider and more an individual whose ideas and beliefs become important even when they differ with those of a biological parent. Basically, well-functioning stepfamilies are similar to well-functioning nuclear families when it comes to making decisions that benefit the individual needs of all family members.

The Role of the Stepparent

Often when people remarry or cohabit, they envision the new mate as a new parent for their children. While a stepparent may provide love, support, financial assistance and guidance to his or her stepchildren, a stepparent is *not* a biological parent and therein lies the problem in many families. The situation becomes even more confusing if the children's biological parent also participates in parenting, even if to a small degree. The relationship is further muddled when an individual is a stepparent to some of the children in a household and a biological parent to others.

How does the stepparent role differ from that of a biological parent? Are there behaviors that are appropriate to biological parenting but inappropriate to stepparenting? Should a stepparent expect the same kind of consideration from stepchildren as he or she does of biological children?

The stepparent role must not be rushed. It takes patience and effort as it develops over a long period of time. The trust of stepchildren is earned when stepparents are consultants, coaches, friends and mediators rather than authority figures or intruders in the children's lives. Here are some options that will help you in creating a happy stepparented family:

• Children must be given time to adjust to the changes that are occurring within the family. They must be able to grieve for their former lives and old relationships.

• If possible, move to a new house or renovate the old house in a way that makes space for new family members to map out their own territory.

• Develop a cordial relationship with your new mate's ex-spouse or partner, as well as the ex-spouse's new partner if there is one, and any grandparents involved in the children's lives. Understand that there is a special bond between a child and his or her biological parents, a bond that must be respected. Be positive and respectful when talking about a stepchild's "other" family.

• Stepparents should learn all they can about the children they live with. And while stepparents and stepchildren should treat each other respectfully, it cannot be expected that they will automatically love each other. A stepparent must openly communicate with stepchildren, peacefully negotiate differences and compromise with them.

• Stepparents should not take on the role of family disciplinarian. Instead they must work to develop a warm, caring relationship with stepchildren and be a good role model. It is best that biological parents handle behavior issues. Attempts to control stepchildren even by warm, communicative stepparents may be resented, especially by adolescents.

• New partners in a stepparenting relationship should be aware of alimony or support orders, estate planning, debts and other legal matters pertaining to the family so there can be no misunderstandings about financial obligations to one family or another.

• Parents in a stepparented family must nurture their own relationship by spending enjoyable time together in private. This can be as simple a thing as going out for coffee together or taking a walk.

• Each parent should spend enjoyable time alone with the children in the family, even if it's an hour a week. This can entail listening to music or reading together, making cookies, going out to lunch or a movie, or just chatting at the kitchen table.

• Schedule a family meeting once a month so that family members can discuss issues and concerns. Remain open to hearing what the children have to say and allow them to be honest about their feelings.

• A stepparent should be positive about all the children in the family. Be sure to compliment them when they deserve it and show appreciation when they do chores or other things that benefit the family.

Creating a happy stepparented family requires continual self-searching and effort on the part of parents, not just at the beginning of the new relationship but every day thereafter. Just as in biological families, or any other kind of family, happiness in a family is created out of knowledge, care, responsibility and respect.

Chapter Eight
CHANGE AND CHALLENGE

"I love you," said a great mother.
"I love you for what you are,
knowing so well what you are.
and I love you more yet, child,
deeper yet than ever, child,
for what you are going to be,
knowing so well you are going far,
knowing your great works are ahead,
ahead and beyond,
yonder and far over yet."

Carl Sandburg
American Poet

When my only child left for college I went through a melancholy period. The house was too quiet, there was no one there to carry the groceries in from the car, I missed our late-night chats, and I now had to walk the dog. Eventually I adjusted to the change and came to enjoy my newfound freedom from child-related chores. The solitude gave me time to read and write more. By the time my son came home from college I was so used to living alone that it took a while to adjust to the noise and social interaction that comes with having a housemate. For two weeks after my son's return I waited up much later than my usual bedtime for him to come home from a date or social outing. Annoyed to find me half asleep (and sometimes sound asleep) in my chair when he wandered in, my son finally said, "Mom, face it, I'm all grown up. Go to bed."

If there is one thing that you can be sure of as a parent it is that just when you get a handle on what is going on with your child, the child changes. You will always be running to catch up with him or her. It is only in understanding what is to come that you stay ahead of the curve. The way in which you accept and handle the normal progressions of your child will help determine the success of each stage of his or her development.

The New World

Nothing astonishes parents more than the dramatic changes that occur in a child's first year of life. This is a period of rapid brain development, resulting in enhanced motor skills, language acquisition and strong emotional attachments. It is at this time that joy and empathy evolve, feelings that bring about happiness and concern for others.

What is most important for parents to understand is how significant early experiences are in shaping the brain development of infants. The regulation of emotions—love, anger, fear, joy, sadness—has been linked to the degree in which parents are loving, responsive and caring. Trauma or emotional deprivation at an early age has lifelong implications because of their effect on the brain's wiring, making it difficult to overcome distressful early experiences, even through psychotherapy.

What children need from parents during their earliest years is physical contact, verbal communication and forms of play that are age-appropriate and in tune with temperament. Here are some of the things that parents can do to stimulate the infant brain in positive ways:

• Just after his birth expose your baby to a low level of stimulation, such as soft music or gentle talk.

• Babies learn about the world through their eyes. At three months they will be attracted to objects in the environment that promote their sensory skills: mobiles, stuffed animals, rattles, picture books and crib toys.

• Speak to your infant often, in animated tones so that they can learn the patterns of language. When talking, turn off the television or radio, and keep distracting noises to a minimum.

• By six months your baby will be interested in how things work. This is when you demonstrate things such as ringing a bell, turning the TV on and off, and turning the water on in the sink. Tell them what happens as a result of these actions, for example, "The doorbell is ringing. Grandma is here."

• At nine months begin helping your baby coordinate the sounds he hears to his motor skills by encouraging him to ring the bell or turn on a light.

• Remember that babbling in this first year of life—speaking in one-syllable combinations such as "ba," "da" and "ma"—is your baby's way of having a conversation with you. Babies also exhibit gestures that help them communicate. As a parent you must promote language development by talking to your baby in a high-pitched voice, using simple sentences. Ask questions (Where's your doll?). Encourage turn-taking (if the baby says "nose" respond with "Yes, that's a pretty nose.").

• Read to your baby, early and often. Very young children like picture books with little or no text. They like repetition, and while you may get tired of reading a particular book, they do not. Young children also like songs and lullabies. Read slowly and have physical contact with your baby when doing so.

• Play with your baby. To do this, go down to her level (sit on the floor, or hold the baby on your lap). Use playpens and other restraints as little as possible. Present new objects one at a time. Call attention to things in the environment: colorful fabrics, a photo, toys. Encourage multi-sensory experiences, linking touch, sight and sound.

• Always be calm and patient. Be sure your activities correspond to where your baby is physically and intellectually.

• Pay close attention to the baby's mood while playing with him. Notice if he has lost interest in playing or is tired. Follow the baby's emotional lead when it comes to play.

Getting Up and Heading Out

The changes that occur in children from 18 months of age until they begin school are enough to make any parent dizzy. Walking has given them a "second birth," one that turns them into very active creatures. New worlds open up to the child who can move easily around the environment, absorbing sights and sounds, touching this and that, experiencing all within grasp. As their muscles develop (body size and shape both change) children gain the ability to run, jump and eventually ride bikes and skate. Four-year-olds love to manage the remote control of the TV and DVD player. By age five they want to dress themselves completely.

The Family Bed Issue

It may be one of the best kept family secrets in America that millions of parents move aside in bed to make room for their babies and toddlers. Parents' reluctance to admit to this sleeping arrangement is due to the strong Western taboo against parent-child bed sharing. Since this is a preference that is not about to end despite the warnings of many pediatricians, it is best that parents understand both the positive and negative aspects of bed sharing. Here are things to consider:

• The family bed provides a feeling of security for the child, and keeps him from feeling lonely or afraid at night.

• A nursing mother or a parent watching over an ailing child will find it easier to take care of an infant during the night.

• Co-sleeping leads to a decrease in children's sleeping problems, such as those caused by bad dreams or nightmares, which are common to about 25 percent of children ages three to eight years.

• Parents often enjoy the closeness they feel with their children when they share a bed. It provides a feeling of family togetherness.

• Children who sleep alone tend to be more dependent on their parents than co-sleepers.

• Co-sleeping makes parents instantly available in cases of emergency. There is evidence that crib deaths are less likely to occur when infants sleep with their parents.

• The family bed keeps people warmer in homes where there is limited heat.

• Some parents prefer to sleep alone, particularly if the child is physically active while sleeping. Sometimes the bed is too small for so much unity.

• Bed sharing interferes with adult sexual activity, although enterprising and creative couples do not find this a problem.

Good judgment must be used when sharing a bed with infants or toddlers. Here are safety tips:

• Obviously do not smoke in bed or anywhere near your child.

• Keep the infant next to his or her mother rather than father. Mothers tend to be more aware of baby's movement and presence. Be sure the baby is on his back, not his stomach.

• Parental drinking or drug use makes bed sharing very risky. It should not be done under these circumstances.

• Do not put your bed next to a wall. If you must, be sure there are no crevices that an infant could suffocate in.

• Do not use fluffy comforters, which can accidentally suffocate a baby. Light blankets are best. Do not put pillows near the baby's head.

• Never sleep with an infant on a water bed or sofa. Use a firm mattress and be sure the headboard and footboard fit properly.

There are other options for parents who want their children close at night but not in their bed. Some parents keep a cradle or small crib in the bedroom. Children who are four and older can curl up in sleeping bags on the floor. For parents who prefer privacy at night, a part of one day a week, such as Saturday morning, can be "sleep together" time. And if there are young siblings in the house, there's always the option of them sleeping together at night.

Like most things when it comes to parenting, the rules are not written in stone. You have to make a decision about the family bed based on your and your child's needs and the situation you find yourselves in. Whether the family bed is for you or not depends on safety issues, parental attitudes, developmental stages, cultural beliefs, family-of-origin experiences and other factors that influence your decision. Rest assured that children can do fine whether they share a bed with parents or sleep alone in their own rooms.

Talking Too Little and Too Much

Children by age two are increasingly able to mentally represent objects or actions they perceive in the environment. This means they can now play make-believe, have imaginary friends, and verbalize what they are thinking.

Language is an agent of thought and as their vocabulary increases children are able to think more clearly and problem-solve more effectively. Between the ages of two and six, language development is rapid. At age two the average child knows 200 words. By age six this has increased to an astonishing 14,000 words for children who have been consistently talked to in early childhood (this comes to about 10 new words a day).

Children talk if they are encouraged to talk. This means parents must engage in two-way conversations with them. The flow of a dialogue with children is maintained through turnabouts, talk that encourages a response. Understand that the meaning of a conversation is unique to the parent and child having that conversation. In other words, when a mother says "good girl," this can have a different meaning than a father's "good girl." Mother's "good girl" may mean, "you are so helpful." A father's "good girl" may mean, "you are so sweet."

There are a number of techniques you can use to promote conversations with your young child. It is a matter of listening carefully and responding in ways that extend the conversation.

- Acknowledging: "That's a good idea." "Very interesting." "You really thought about that."

- Restating: "Does that mean ...?" "It sounds to me like you want to go there."

- Clarifying: "Tell me more about that." "I'm not sure I know what you mean."

- Disagreeing: "What do you think about this idea?"

- Expanding: "What else do you think we can do?" "Do you have any more ideas about that?"

Rules of the Road

When children are to go out into the world they must learn how to act in ways that benefit them and keep them from having problems with others. There are things that it is advantageous for them to know, particularly when it comes to self-regulatory behaviors.

Safety Issues: It is essential that you familiarize your children with dangerous things. While you don't want to terrify them about the world, there are concerns, such as street traffic, strangers and dangerous items in the environment. Be careful not to encourage their fears with talk of the "boogie man" and other imaginary characters. Separate your own fears (dogs, cats, the dark, etc.) from truly unsafe forces. Try not to hoist your own worries on your children.

Routines serve children well by giving structure to their lives. While schedules don't have to be rigid, it is best that children know when it is time to eat their meals, brush their teeth, take a bath, do homework and go to bed. As a part of their mealtime routine children should learn to eat properly with utensils, and have good table manners.

Self-care: Young children can dress themselves, keep themselves clean, tidy their rooms, and care for their possessions. It is helpful for them to learn to do little chores, such as finding items at the supermarket. This makes them feel useful and competent.

Manners: Young children often have trouble with self-regulation. They must learn not to interrupt when someone is on the phone or engaged in conversation. (They can be taught to say "excuse me" if it is important.) "Thank you" is another term of politeness important for children to know.

Respect: Early on children do well by respecting others, which can mean anything from being helpful to another person to not taking things that don't belong to them, such as a friend's toy. Respect for others is primarily learned in the home, by watching how parents treat their friends, neighbors and relatives.

Another Step Forward

Family life changes for parents when children begin school. One of my friends plunged into a surprising depression when her first-born started first grade; another went blissfully back to work after having been a stay-at-home mother.

Middle childhood is an especially busy (and exhausting) time for family members as children join sports teams, sing in the school play, need help with homework, have birthday parties and go on school trips. For working parents there is the worry about after-school time, and enough time. It takes effort to keep a degree of intimacy in the parental relationship at this point but it is important that parents find the time to be alone with each other and enjoy themselves. Single parents have the additional stress of raising children while pursuing relationships outside the family.

It is the task of parents at this juncture to help their children interpret the world outside the home, to assist them in meeting the demands of school and to teach them to manage the stresses and disappointments they will inevitably encounter as they venture forth.

The Importance of Competence

The key to success in middle childhood is the development of competence, a set of skills that will lead them to success in life. It is during this period that children come to believe in their ability to initiate activities, learn new things and accomplish their goals.

Competence depends upon social setting. A young boy living in Anchorage, Alaska, might strive to become skilled at fishing while a New York City youngster hopes to master the Internet on his computer. Children now become "workers" within their cultural group, winning recognition by producing things. A sense of achievement and success becomes the key to developing, a positive self-image.

During this stage of development, children establish the work habits that will carry them through life. They develop a view of themselves that will affect their future choices and relationships. It is here that parental attitudes toward children make children feel "good" or "bad" about themselves.

If you see your child as smart and capable, she will develop a positive self-concept, one that will propel her to continue working hard toward her goals. If you tend to be judgmental and unaccepting of your child's abilities, she is apt to feel inadequate, which can lead her to become overly dependent on you. Her sense of worthlessness may even lead to feelings of hostility, aggressiveness, and the desire to strike out at others.

It is essential that you show, by word and deed, how important school and learning is. This means talking positively about school, cooperating with teachers, and attending school events. Parents must also make sure that their child's educational experience is a positive one, which means the school she attends must promote her intellect and abilities.

Since learning skills such as reading, writing and language proficiency are so important at this stage, you must stay aware of your child's progress in these areas. If you see a problem you must face it right away, head on. Is your child reading at grade level? Does she need extra help? If there is a language problem is it caused by a hearing problem?

Because competence is such an important domain of self-esteem, you must help your child identify her particular areas of aptitude. There are lots of possibilities: Does she draw well? Is she an excellent reader? Are her motor skills exceptional? Can she design Web sites? Does she write interesting poems? Find something she is good at. Enroll her in an art class. Take her to the library as often as possible. Give her music lessons. Send her writings to relatives. Visit museums. Attend concerts. In American society we tend to value athletic abilities above all other talents but, in fact, other skills and interests are just as important and should be encouraged.

Making Comparisons

School-age children evaluate their abilities, attractiveness, competency level, and opinions by comparing themselves to others. They rely on social reality, an understanding of how other people act, think, feel and view the world. In doing so, they develop a social self, a sense of who they are in relationship to the people around them.

Although young children make comparisons, it is at about age eight or nine that this sensitivity to others increases dramatically, primarily because children are so often with peers. You can learn a lot about a child by noting who she compares herself to. In general, children in high-achievement schools often look to more academically successful peers for comparison, which sometimes leads high-achievers to doubt themselves. Those in low-achievement schools tend to compare themselves to peers who are doing worse academically as a way to protect themselves from feeling like failures.

What can you do to help your child become competent? How can she be encouraged to develop skills?

• Let your child know that she has the potential to do most of the things she wants in life if she is willing to work hard. Do not discourage her by being critical of her abilities, personality or motivation.

• Help your child discover what she is most interested in and has the potential to do well. Be realistic about her abilities. It doesn't do much good to encourage a child in something she is clearly not suited for or doesn't like. Differentiate between what your child is really interested in and what you want her to be interested in.

• Praise your child for specific accomplishments, such as "I like the way you helped Roger with his reading" or "You wrote a lovely poem." This says more to a child than "you are a nice girl" or "you are smart."

• Be clear that accomplishments take time and hard work. Tell your child that success is relative to the effort she puts into something. Point out those people in history or the news, such as champion cyclist Lance Armstrong, who achieved after great effort.

• Let your child know that taking a risk can be a good thing. If she tries something new and different the end result might lead to an exciting opportunity or plain enjoyment.

• Encourage your child to ask questions about the things that interest her. Do not teach her to be a passive learner, one who relies on her teachers to present her with facts. Be open to her questioning you, and even disagreeing with you.

• Emphasize the importance of getting a good education. Be positive when talking about or dealing with teachers. Do not set up an adversarial relationship with school authorities. If there are problems, show your child how they can be solved in diplomatic ways.

• Teach your child to take responsibility for her actions. Discourage her from blaming teachers, friends, siblings and others for her errors. Do not harp on mistakes or failures but rather help your child correct an error or choose a better course of action in the future.

• Teach your child to be proud of herself when she gets a good grade, performs well, helps at home and otherwise accomplishes something. Allow her to accept responsibility for this success. Do not distract from it with comments or judgments that diminish the achievement.

• Explain the importantance of long-term planning on future success. Give examples from your own life of how planning and delayed gratification led to an accomplishment.

Creating Hardy Children

Life is stressful for everyone but some children are more resilient than others. They have a psychological hardiness about them, that is, an ability to cope well when things gets difficult. As a parent, it is important that you help your child meet the changes and challenges of life in positive ways. In an age where far too many children are being treated for depression, it is up to you to help your child envision a bright and productive future.

Children learn how to handle stress or difficulty from their parents. They see how their parents act when they are in a minor car accident or lose something or don't get a desired promotion. If a parent is negative, fearful or pessimistic about life, a child will tend to be that way also.

It is particularly important for you to assess situations accurately so that your child can learn to do so also. Don't make a cold into pneumonia. A rainy day while on vacation is not a disaster, it's weather. A traffic tie-up is a traffic tie-up, what can you do? (This is an opportunity to chat with your child.) If you are dramatic about every little thing that happens, your child will be, too.

There are ways to promote resiliency in your children.

• Help your child see that most setbacks and unfortunate life events are temporary and that life will be good again after a hard time. Let her know that life never runs smoothly all the time, but the difference in people is how they handle the tough times. Turn "I'm never going to play the guitar" into "I need to work harder so I can play the guitar."

• Let your child know that a failure in one area does not necessarily generalize to another. "I'm terrible in sports" is a far different attitude than "I'm not good at basketball."

• Never get into a "blaming game" with your child, making her feel that it is something about her personally that causes misfortunes. Chronic self-blaming and guilt are the ingredients of depression. "If you weren't so clumsy you wouldn't have knocked that glass over" serves only to make a child feel badly. Help your child understand that annoying and unfortunate things happen in life, no matter who a person is.

• Show your children that there is a Plan B and Plan C and so on when something doesn't work out as expected. There is usually another way to solve a problem or handle a situation.

• Do not scare your child with talk of all the terrible things that can happen to her in the world. You can discuss not talking to strangers, or how to cross the street carefully, but there is no need to scare a child half to death because of your own anxiety.

• Do interesting and somewhat adventurous things with your child. Go into cities, introduce her to people unlike herself, take in a concert, travel to exciting places.

• Do not smother or overprotect your child. You can't be with her every minute; therefore, you must teach her to cope with life as it unfolds.

In the course of growing up, children have to deal with many changes, to their selves and in the outside world. As a parent, your attitude and handling of changes influences how equipped your child will be in adapting to and thriving to life's comings and goings.

We want our children to have lives filled with friendship and love and high deeds. We want them to be eager to learn and be willing to confront challenges. We want our children to be grateful for what they receive from us, but to be proud of their own accomplishments. We want them to grow up with confidence in the future, a love of adventure, a sense of justice, and courage enough to act on that sense of justice. We want them to be resilient in the fact of the setbacks and failures that growing up always brings. And when the time comes, we want them to be good parents.

Martin Seligman
Learned Optimism

Chapter Nine
THE SOCIAL CONTRACT

"Call me Daddy."

"Only babies call their fathers Daddy."

"Then I'm not going to call you Daddy either," Chandler said.

"I like being called Daddy. It makes me feel adored. Girls, I want to ask you a question and I want you to answer with brutal honesty. Don't spare Daddy's feelings, just tell me what you think from the heart."

Jennifer rolled her eyes and said, "Oh, Dad, not this game again."

I said, "Who is the greatest human being you've encountered on this earth?"

"Mama," Lucy answered quickly, grinning at her father.

"Almost right," I replied. "Now let's try it again. Think of the most splendid, wonderful person you personally know. The answer should spring to your lips."

"You!" Chandler shouted.

"An angel. A pure, snow-white angel, and so smart. What do you want, Chandler? Money? Jewels? Furs? Stocks and bonds? Ask anything, darling, and your loving Daddy will get it for you."

Pat Conroy
The Prince of Tides

The singer Carly Simon has often spoken of her painful shyness as a child and of her feelings of inferiority when she compared herself to her two older sisters. In response to family turmoil she developed a serious stutter and a number of fears and phobias, which kept her nearly incapacitated socially. Her mother advised Carly to sing out when she couldn't speak out, which led the talented child to put her energy into writing songs. One of them exclaims, "Oh, but to be; oh, but to be; oh. But to be; I'd like to be my older sister."

Much of children's contentment as adults will come from interpersonal relationships, so parents must set the groundwork for such interactions. If a child does not have a degree of social competence by six or seven, she will suffer throughout her school age years and possibly into adulthood. When a child goes out into the world it is important that she have the social skills that will enable her to make and keep friends, develop loving relationships, and get along well with co-workers and other people she comes in contact with. Not everyone is as blessed as Carly Simon, with enough talent to compensate for social deficiencies, therefore it is important that parents help their children navigate the complex world of social relationships.

To adequately comprehend their social environment children must decode social cues. They must watch others' body language, listen to tones of voice, interpret social cues, recognize what the body language or voice means, search for a response, figure out an appropriate reaction to the social situation, mentally select a particular response and then act in an appropriate way. To keep friendships they must be able to understand another's point of view and accept differences that arise as a result. They have to be truthful and loyal and be able to handle conflict and frustration.

How social children are is partly determined by genetics—some youngsters are shyer or quieter than others—but the basic skills of social behavior are primarily learned at home. Time spent in a good day-care center or with people who have positive social relationships also contribute to skill in this area.

Picking Up Signals

Infancy is primarily about forming social-emotional attachments. It is the task of parents to see that their baby feels loved and nurtured. This period is built on a lot of holding and hugging. It's about feeding an infant when he is hungry, changing him when he is wet and allowing the baby to sleep as much as is needed without noise or other annoyances disturbing him. What an infant must feel at this early stage of life is a sense of trust. The child must see the world as a safe and caring place. The rewards a parent gets for being attentive to a baby's needs are smiles, open arms, and generally cheerful interactions, even with difficult children.

From the minute they are born children send out messages (I'm hungry, I'm tired, I want to be cuddled) and parents must learn to read these messages properly. Before they can speak children signal what they need by cooing, smiling, crying, drooling, gesturing, grasping and babbling. This is the beginning of forming the emotional attachments that will carry them through life. How attuned parents are to what their child wants or needs determines to a large extent what the child's relationship with parents and others will be as she grows up.

Knowledge and Experience Go Hand in Hand

Reading an infant's cues properly comes from experience and an understanding of childhood developmental levels. Crying, for example, is a signaling behavior that changes as a child ages, requiring different responses as time goes by.

During the first six months of life, crying is an attempt to get physical or psychological needs met. A baby will cry if he is hungry, cold, hot and in other ways uncomfortable. As he gets older, he will cry if he is afraid or frustrated. At some point during the first year of life, he may cry at the sight of a stranger or when a parent is out of sight. While some crying is necessary for normal physiological function and tension reduction, a baby's cries should never be ignored. Babies cry less if they are consistently held and comforted when they are upset. This also adds to their sense of safety and security. It leads to a secure attachment, an emotional connectedness that will carry them through life. Children who are securely attached to their parents are fairly easy to spot. They laugh easily, enjoy playing games and are interested in the people and world around them.

If a parent is inconsistent in responding to a child and vacillates between meeting his needs and tuning him out, the parent might get a whiny, clingy youngster on her hands, one who is unsure about his feelings for his parent. While he may fuss and plead to get attention, he may also become angry and reject of those closest to him.

It is not always easy for a parent to know if his or her child is experiencing emotional problems. A client in my therapy practice, a single mother, had a four-year-old son who avoided contact with her. He did not stop playing with his toys when she came in from work and asked him for a kiss hello. He rarely made eye contact with her and turned his body away from her when she held him. After talking to the mother a while I discovered that she hurried him through breakfast in the morning before driving him to a babysitter's house. She was often very tired when she got home from work and was unable to meet her son's needs. When he whined or fussed she put him in his room. She kept peanut butter, jelly, bread and other food on a bottom shelf of the refrigerator so that he could get dinner for himself. The mother thought it was terrific that her son could put himself to bed. "He's the most independent child I've ever known," she bragged to me. I told her it seemed to me that the boy no longer relied on her for emotional support, and in his disappointment protected himself psychologically by not having contact with her. What was interpreted as independence and autonomy was, in actuality, a lack of trust and an inability to share in a close relationship. The child was saying, "I don't need anyone" as a way to defend against his disappointment and pain.

Fun and Games

Children become social creatures by playing. Whether spontaneous and unstructured, or organized and controlled, play teaches children to share, cooperate and resolve conflicts. Play also helps children learn gender rules and expectations, and it enhances intellectual development.

In infancy children love interpersonal play, which involves face-to-face interactions, social games, or routines. If you stick your tongue out at a baby he will do the same. Word games like "this little piggy went to market" which entail touching the baby's toes, usually brings squeals of delight. Very soon infants enjoy object play, the investigation of objects and materials, such as blocks or dolls.

When playing with a baby parents must be attuned to changes in his mood. An infant might enjoy being bounced on a parent's knee for a while but can tire of this game and become cranky. The crankiness is a cue that the game should end.

By age two, children enjoy symbolic play, which is less dependent on parental interaction. Now children engage in pretend play. They answer toy telephones and imitate television characters. As hard as it may be to accept, most children are now more interested in playing with other children than with their parents. They especially prefer same-sex playmates because of shared interests.

It is in middle childhood that children begin to truly venture away from the family and their parents and move toward peer-group activities. Those who engage in friendships with children of the opposite gender tend to be more positive in their social interactions and more cooperative with each other.

Between the ages of six and 12 children spend almost half their time in the company of peers, children approximately their own age. In this new context they set out to discover who they are outside of their family setting. The sense of self they have at home—where adults define who children are and dictate how they should behave—gives way to another self, one that develops from the interaction with new friends and acquaintances. The boy who is withdrawn and quiet at home might well be the class cutup at school. The studious young girl might turn into a star lacrosse player under the influence of peers.

Best Friends

Children who are liked by their peers are those who tend to be positive and happy, and possessing of a good sense of humor. They are self-confident but not conceited, they care about others, are good listeners, and they show enthusiasm for their companions. They generally take their playmates' views and desires into consideration when making a decision about an idea or activity. When they have conversations with others, they alternatively talk and listen. Well-liked children are generally reliable and honest. They are supportive of their friends and tend to like other children like themselves. They stay in control of their emotions and they are nonaggressive in their interactions.

About 10 percent of school-age children are disliked and rejected by their peers; they are rarely considered anyone's best friend. This is because they tend to be aggressive, impulsive, or disruptive. In their relationships with peers they are often domineering, bossy or insulting. They are sometimes dishonest and not likely to keep confidences. Their values and interests often differ from those of their peers.

A smaller group of children are neither liked nor disliked by their peers but they are generally neglected as close friends. This may be the result of their personalities, in that they prefer solitary activities or are shy, or it can be because they are not well cared for by their parents, which sets them apart from their peers. I vividly recall bright and pleasant twin boys in my son's third grade class who came to school so dirty and disheveled that their classmates shied away from them.

Rejection by one's peers is a devastating circumstance for children and the effects of this kind of relationship linger into adulthood. It can lead to excessive absences from school and early dropout, delinquency in adolescence and behavior problems. Unpopular children often have low self-esteem and suffer from depression and other mental health problems. For this reason, parents must take an honest look at their children's relationships with others, with a goal of helping them develop the social skills needed to attract other people into their lives. Here are some of the things you might ask yourself:

• Does my child participate in group activities? Does he play by the rules of the group?

• How does my child deal with conflict? What does he do when he gets angry?

• What does my child do when he doesn't get his way with peers?

• How helpful is my child in social situations?

• Is my child polite and considerate when in public? Does he have good table manners?

• Can my child maintain a give and take in conversations with his friends? Is he respectful of ideas or opinions other than his own?

• How does my child cope with being teased? Does he have a good sense of humor? Does he laugh and have a good time when appropriate?

• Does my child stand up for himself when being bullied or mistreated? Does he assert his rights when need be?

• How does my child request things? What is his tone like when talking to others?

• How does my child handle failure? What happens when he is frustrated?

• Does my child tell the truth when talking to friends? Is he loyal? Can he keep confidences?

The Friendly Home

Home is where children acquire the emotional base needed for venturing into the world in search of friendship and peer contact. It is here that they learn the schemes by which positive relationships are formed. You must help your child interpret and respond appropriately in social situations by providing him with ways to enhance his social skills. There are a number of ways to do this:

• Present your child with opportunities to play with and interact with other children, particularly in pleasant environments. Children who experience numerous shifts in peer group membership have more difficulty developing social strategies than those who remain with the same friends over a long period.

• Play with your child and have fun with him. Do peer-like things, such as playing ball or board games. Always be positive and fair when playing with your child. Never encourage cheating to win a game.

• Smile and laugh often during play and refrain from criticizing or controlling your child when he is enjoying himself.

• Listen to your child's suggestions and ideas about play activities. Teach him participation skills. Show him how to begin an activity and involve all the players, stay with a game or activity until the end, wait his turn, stay calm whether ahead or behind, and be a good winner or good loser.

• Talk to your child about his behavior with regard to friends. While driving in the car, walking down the street, over lunch, or during a shopping excursion, you have opportunities to chat with your child about his friend-ships. It is important for you to show you are interested in your child's social life and possible problems without prying too much, giving strong, unsolicited opinions, or unwanted lectures that shut your child down. Teach him to take an interest in others, and to listen and respond appropriately when having a conversation.

• Teach your child to take a problem-solving approach to his friendships. When he is upset about a relationship or has questions about a friend, let him come up with suggestions or solutions to the problem. Instead of telling him what to do, listen to him and support his efforts. Do not trivialize issues or tell him what to do when he tells you something about a friend.

• Teach your child the strategies needed to be a friend and have friends. Help him learn to compromise, take turns, express himself without arguing, negotiate differ-ences and play fairly. Also help him understand the rules of conversation, such as not interrupting when someone is speaking or not bragging in a way that makes others feel inferior.

• An important part of friendship is the ability to feel empathy for others—in effect, put oneself in another's place and vicariously experience his or her emotions. Help your child recognize the effect of his behavior on others.

• Treat your child's friends respectfully. Make them feel welcome in your home. Do not insult your child's friends or act rudely toward them. If a friend does something you do not like, focus on the behavior and not on the child's personality. If you are too critical of your child's friends you may find your child spending more time at his friends' homes than his own.

• When possible, limit your child's exposure to rudeness, violence and other types of unacceptable social behavior, be it through television or movies, and even by adults in the family. Through your own behavior show your child how to treat other people respectfully.

• Work at keeping your personal relationships peaceful and respectful. Be sure that the adults in the family behave in caring and polite ways toward each other. While it is common for siblings to argue, do not allow them to be mean or hurtful toward each other.

Chapter Ten
LETTING GO AND HOLDING ON

I dreamt the other night that she had left on a trip around the world but that I had forgotten to pack her bag. In the dream it was clothes and toothpaste and shoes that I had sent her off without, but when I woke up I knew it was the less tangible things that concerned me: common sense, the ability to resist peer pressure, respect for herself and for others, focus, the courage to meet life's challenges, and the courage to love, to become attached to another human being. All the things that all mothers and fathers worry about. All the things that cannot possibly be packed at the last minute. Are they in the suitcase or not? How do we ever know? When do we know? Now that I was so completely attached to this child, I was having a hard time letting her go.

Susan Allport
A Natural History of Parenting

When CNN reporter Geraldo Rivera was in high school he realized that social standing segregated his classmates, with the athletes, cheerleaders and college-bound kids at the top. Feeling insecure because of his mixed Jewish-Hispanic background he took to hanging out with a street gang called the Corner Boys, whose main occupation was sipping beer through a straw. When he was 14 Geraldo discovered girls—and sex. From then on he made sure he had more than one amorous relationship going at a time. Years later, after a few failed marriages, Geraldo admitted that he treated women badly, and he came to see that his undervaluing of them was learned from his father, who was unfaithful to

Geraldo's mother throughout their marriage. At points in his life Geraldo lied about his name, nationality and background in an effort to overcome his feelings of social inferiority. During his career he was infamous for having temper tantrums and being difficult to work with. It took him well into middle age to finally settle down emotionally, commit to a marriage and fatherhood, and earn the professional recognition he craved.

The bridge that carries children through high school and into adulthood—adolescence—is a passage that is difficult whether children grow up in troubled homes like Geraldo's or in well-functioning families. This stage of development, beginning on average at 8–10 for girls and 12–14 for boys, can last from 6 years to 12 years, (yes, that's right, 12 years) but in any case a child should emerge from this period as a caring, contented, productive adult.

In early adolescence, before age 16, the most obvious changes are physical. This a time when a dramatic increase in the production of sex hormones leads to the ability to reproduce. This rush of hormonal activity can provoke wide mood swings, taking an adolescent from a state of joy to one of discontent in a short period of time, with no obvious cause.

In mid-adolescence, ages 13–16 for girls and 14-20 for boys, friendship and peer relationships become most important. This is the time of greatest parent-child conflict, as children become more sexual and challenge their parents' authority.

Late adolescence, from about 17–25, sees a decrease in tensions as parent-child relationships become more adult-like. By now children are focused on discovering who they are and where they want to go, and they are engaged in developing intimate relationships outside the family.

Some cultures have rites that mark the shift from childhood to adulthood but generally American culture ignores this major transition, unless you consider obtaining a driver's license or a first legal alcoholic drink a ceremony. The reason children become so wrapped up in driving, drinking, smoking and the like is because they view these activities as signs of being grown up.

Understanding Adolescence

Adolescence can tax the patience of even the best parent, but it is particularly stressful for those parents who do not understand what their children are going through. A sweet and energetic son may become moody and difficult. He stays up late at night and has to be nagged (and sometimes dragged) from bed in the morning and pushed off to school. A daughter who once got straight A's loses interest in school and becomes obsessed with her appearance. Her bedroom looks like a war has been fought in it. What in the world is happening here? Nothing that isn't normal and manageable—with knowledge, deep breaths, and a lot of patience.

Informed parents recognize that they no longer have complete authority over their adolescent children. They know that teenagers bring new friendships and different ideas and values into a family's life. These parents are aware that the way children distinguish themselves from their parents' generation is through their music, clothing styles, cultural icons and even language. If you are open to what your child is experiencing you can learn from him and add interest to your life. My own son and I landed on common ground when, at 17, he introduced me to the Dave Matthews Band. I, in turn, dragged out my old Bob Dylan tapes (which he doesn't yet appreciate).

The notion that parents must "survive" their children's adolescence is a media invention, as most adolescents are good kids who do their best and get along well with their parents. The discontent many parents feel when their children go through adolescence is less a result of the children's actions then it is of watching these fun-loving, energetic, physically active youngsters head out into the world at a time when parents are confronted with the wrinkles, aches, waning sex lives and disappointments that often mark middle age.

Other parental issues can interfere with the optimal development of adolescent children. Parents who feel pressured at work tend to be less accepting of their children and more impatient at home. In single-parent families in which there are financial problems, conflict increases. Parents who are depressed due to unemployment or personal problems are harder on their children and punish them more than parents whose lives are easier.

The Beginning

A rapid increase in height and weight, known as the adolescent growth spurt, first hits girls at about 10 years of age and boys at about 12, and it lasts approximately two years, resulting in sexual maturity. Because of gender differences it is not uncommon to find that sixth grade girls in the United States are significantly taller than most of the boys in their class. On average, boys begin to overtake girls in height and weight by age 14. During this period almost all skeletal and muscular components change, but not uniformly. Even the eyes grow, which leads to nearsightedness in one-fourth of adolescents, an important fact for parents to know if their children begin to have difficulty in school or are going to get a driver's licenses a few years down the road.

This is a most difficult time for children as their out-of-proportion body parts lead to an embarrassing gawkiness in appearance. Children now eat and sleep more, and they sometimes have aches and pains from their body's growth process. Adolescent girls often complain of headaches, stomachaches, backaches, anxiety and a general feeling of tiredness and feeling "down." Because of the cultural emphasis on female attractiveness, adolescent girls are at risk of developing eating disorders, depression and other mental health problems. Parents must also pay attention for signs of steroid use in boys and other extreme methods of body molding.

Some Are Early, Some Are Late

Children of exactly the same age can appear years apart in physical development and psychological maturity, therefore it is important for parents to be aware of the way the timing of maturation affects a child psychologically and socially. If parents have an understanding of the reason behind a child's crankiness, tiredness, mood changes and such, it makes them better able to help their child through this stage of development.

Early maturing boys are larger, stronger and better coordinated than others their age, which gives them a heightened sense of self-esteem. Because of this they tend to be more relaxed and good-natured than later maturing boys. They are often better in sports than their peers and somewhat intellectually advanced. Socially they are likely to be leaders and because of their popularity tend to date earlier. Often parents and teachers treat early maturing boys as if they are more grown up than they actually are. In some cases early maturers are denied the opportunity that later maturing adolescents have to slowly integrate the stressors that result from development during this period.

Early maturing girls have a far different experience than early maturing boys. The girls tend to stand out from their peers, and they often feel uncomfortably "different" by virtue of being taller and more physically developed than others their age. As a result they are more likely to be psychologically distressed then their later developing classmates. For some, this earlier sexuality attracts as-yet unwanted attention from older boys while others welcome this increased popularity.

Boys who are late maturers are sometimes perceived by adults as being less competent and less likely to achieve than their more mature peers. They tend to have greater feelings of insecurity and inadequacy, worry more about rejection, have more conflicts within their own families, are self-conscious, and have a poorer self-concept.

Late maturing girls have the advantage of reaching puberty the same time as many of their male peers, which helps in maintaining friendships. Late maturers are less likely to have academic problems and are more likely to conform to their parents' expectations. Of all groups, late maturing girls show the highest achievement levels.

Daily Rhythms

Adolescents need eight to nine hours of sleep a night and sometimes more when the growth spurt begins. Because of hormonal changes, they stay up late at night and consequently need more sleep in the morning, yet oddly enough, school systems around the country force their oldest students to work against their normal biological rhythms. Sleep deprivation can cause symptoms of depression, poor concentration, irritability and increased stress. A lack of proper rest is a major cause of problems in school.

In today's society many adolescents eat high-calorie foods that are unhealthy, and they engage in relatively little physical activity. Parents must be aware of their children's dietary needs and provide food that is both nutritious and healthy. They must place emphasis on the need for healthy foods, such as fruit and vegetables, and limit the amount of "junk food" and sugary sodas kept in the house.

Adolescents should engage in some kind of exercise, such as walking or a sports activity, at least three times a week. This will help in bone and muscle growth, control weight, and reduce anxiety. If possible, family members should find mutually satisfying physical activities to participate in together, be it bike riding, hiking, going to a gym or just taking walks together. Here is a good opportunity for parents to spend enjoyable time with their children.

Whether parents approve or not, a significant number of adolescents experiment sexually, more than half by age 17. It is a reality of life and parents would be wise to recognize this. Heightened feelings of sexuality leads some adolescents to watch sexually-explicit movies or televisions shows, read magazines or books that have sexual themes, tell sex-related jokes, and use unpleasant language.

Of those youngsters who have sexual partners, up to half do not use birth control regularly when engaging in sexual intercourse, which is why more than 10 percent of births in the United States are to unmarried adolescents. It is especially important that children understand the long-term implications of sexual activity. Moralizing about sex and trying to make children feel guilty about it are not particularly effective techniques in delaying such activity. It is more helpful to concentrate on the practical considerations of engaging in sex at a young age—pregnancy and its long-term effects on schooling and occupational opportunities and the potential for diseases. Remember, adolescence can be a long stretch of time and it is not realistic to assume children will not experiment sexually, particularly between ages 16 to 25. It is the responsibility of parents to provide their adolescent children with accurate information about sex, birth control and sexually transmitted diseases. Parents lose credibility when they present false facts about sex. Educating children about sex does not mean you are giving their child permission to engage in sexual behavior; rather, it enables them to make wise decisions in this regard.

Strange Thoughts

When he was 17 years old my son drove his best friend home from a party. A police officer spotted the friend relaxing in the passenger's seat of the car, drinking a beer (an illegal act in my hometown). As a result, my son lost his driver's license for six months and was ordered to do 40 hours of community service (he weeded the gardens around a local hospital and ended up covered with poison ivy). I was annoyed but not surprised that my son had been so foolish, given the research on the adolescent brain and the tendency of teenagers to do seemingly stupid things. In fact, I was relieved his offense was not worse and thrilled that he wouldn't be driving for a while.

At one time it was thought that brain development ended at about age 12, but it is now known that throughout the adolescent years and into the early 20s the brain changes in very profound ways due to the building of new neural connections, particularly in the prefrontal cortex, the part of the brain responsible for complex thinking, problem-solving, decision-making, planning, the control of emotions, and the use of language. It is the prefrontal cortex that enables people to prioritize, consider the consequences of actions, control impulses and conform to social expectations.

Since the prefrontal cortex is somewhat underdeveloped in adolescents, a more emotional and instinctive part of the brain called the amygdala often dominants their thinking. These intense biological changes make the adolescent brain especially susceptible to environmental experiences, so much so that stress, neglect, trauma or abuse have a long-term negative impact that is difficult to overcome.

While this shifting brain chemistry often makes adolescents seem restless, moody, talkative and impulsive, be assured that the majority of youngsters get through this stage of development successfully, usually with the understanding and guidance of parents who recognize what their children are going through and do not overreact to what is normal adolescent behavior.

It is during this period of brain growth that children become capable of looking at problems in many ways and exploring a number of solutions. They now think in hypothetical ways, which means they can ponder "what if" or "suppose that…" They are able to conceptualize and plan for the future. It is at this point in development that children develop an ideal and compare it to reality, which means that when parents, teachers and government officials teach one thing but act another way adolescents become disillusioned and cynical. This is also a time when adolescents broaden their view of the world and sometimes feel overwhelmed by its problems. Many ponder the meaning of life and feel confused about this philosophical concept. They fantasize a lot and tend to be idealistic if they haven't yet faced the harsher realities of adult responsibilities. Their idealism makes them critical of parents and others who don't live up to their romantic notions. This new ability to think abstractly enables adolescents to fantasize about the world and themselves and imagine both as they wish them to be.

The World As Me

As children transition from middle childhood to adolescence, they develop a way of thinking termed adolescent egocentrism. Child psychologist David Elkind has described three characteristics of adolescent egocentrism that parents should be aware of:

The *imaginary audience* is a function of adolescent self-consciousness and a preoccupation with their own looks and behavior to the point that they believe everyone around them is as equally interested in them. This self-centeredness makes them feel special, and this often leads to a sense that "nobody understands me." This preoccupation with them-

Your Kids, Their Lives

selves and a fear of not measuring up to their peers cause many adolescents to go through a period of shyness, which leads to isolation from others. Shyness generally lessens as they develop the social skills that bring them friendships.

Most frightening to parents is the adolescent *personal fable*, a perception adolescents have that they are special to the point of being invincible and not subject to natural laws like everyone else. It is why a daughter insists, "nothing is going to happen to me" when she is not permitted to go to a concert in a dangerous part of the city. Because of the personal fable teenagers experiment with drugs, thinking that they can stop whenever they choose to; have unprotected sex because they believe they cannot get a disease or pregnant; or drive too fast and assume that they will not get a ticket. This kind of thinking allows them to weave personal stories or tales of heroism, greatness, or good fortune around themselves to make themselves seem powerful and avoid feelings of insecurity or failure.

We need only listen on a Friday night to adolescents on the telephone trying to figure out where to go to recognize how indecisive they can be. Their lack of prioritizing and difficulty in choosing from many options has been called *pseudostupidity*, a result of overthinking an issue. Even the brightest and most creative of youngsters can sometimes confound parents by showing a marked lapse in judgment. A common result of this kind of thinking leads adolescents to oversimplify or misinterpret situations.

Creating An Identity

When my son was in college I often joked that he was on the four-college, eight-year plan. This is because he changed

134

schools and curriculum a number of times before finally getting a degree in something that interested him. This is not an unusual scenario among adolescents who are trying to figure out who they are, where they come from, and what they want to do with their lives, a process called identity formation. Psychologists place strong emphasis on identity formation because adult intimate relationships, participation in family life, the choice of an occupation or career, coping abilities, motivation, and the development of beliefs and values are shaped by a person's sense of self.

The route to forming an identity differs from child to child. Some youngsters are clear about where they're going. Often they follow a life plan their parents map out for them. Dad was a firefighter and a teenage boy sees himself in this mold. Three generations of a family go to law school and a 16-year-old-girl imagines herself on the Supreme Count.

Many adolescents in today's complex world go through a period of exploring options and alternatives. These youngsters bounce ideas about the future off of family, friends and teachers. They generally have a good sense of self and a flexibility that enables them to eventually figure out who they are and what they want to do with their lives. They make take up the guitar at age 14 and give it up at 15, play one sport and then another, or try their hand at a different jobs while in high school. Some go to college, leave for a while and go back, travel across the country, try different occupations, or take up hobbies that interest them. This is a normal part of testing options in the world. Parents should be realistic about their adolescent's interests and aptitudes. Not every child is suited to go to college. The occupation a parent promotes may not suit a child's personality. If given the chance, adolescents figure out for themselves what they are best suited for in the future.

Unfortunately, there are youngsters who are unable to explore meaningful options in terms of personal beliefs or occupational possibilities. They seem to be aimless, taking up whatever comes along. These adolescents often have low self-esteem and a poor self-image. Their unhappiness may move them from one set of peers to another, and their anxiety may lead them to the excitement and distraction of drugs, alcohol, and risky behavior.

An adolescent's ability to form a positive identity is partly influenced by parental attitudes. Parents who allow their children to think for themselves and be part of the family decision-making process generally foster a positive sense of self in their children. Parents who offer little advice or guidance may raise children who are unable to set goals for the future. Detached, rejecting, neglecting or unengaged parents often produce school dropouts and youngsters who feel aimless. Some adolescents find that a negative identity is easier to live with than none at all. Membership in a gang, cult or totalitarian movement is an act of defense against this confusion.

A Reflection of Self

When my son was an adolescent I encouraged him to join a neighborhood basketball team and form a rock band. Over the years, during summers, I sent him to an adventure camp in Pennsylvania, a film program in Vermont, and a music school in Boston. My goal during the months he was out of school was to put him in the company of adolescents who were learning things rather than just hanging out.

Adolescents have a lot of discretionary time on their hands, most of which is spent with peers. While they must choose their own friends, parents can influence these choices by the resources they provide. Friendships are formed among people who are in close proximity to each other. Even if money is limited, with a little effort, parents can steer their children toward healthy peer environments by finding out what kind of positive activities are available through city recreation departments, religious organizations, foundations and other entities involved with social planning.

It is important for parents to be drawn into this because adolescent identity is often found in the social context of clubs, gangs, cliques, and other groups that children seek membership in. Immersing oneself into a group provides adolescents with a set of ready-made values, which offers a kind of comfort, and quiets some of the anxieties and tensions that come with being an adolescent. In high school, students pick up labels such as "jocks," "druggies," "populars," "brains," "nerds," and "weirdos," and peers gravitate toward one or another group because members have shared beliefs, attitudes, and interests. Students who do well in school tend to be friends with other high-achieving students, and sports-oriented kids like to be with other athletes. It is not so much that peers influence a child but rather that alike-thinking youngsters find each other. Parents can learn a lot about their children by looking at the people they hang around with.

Parents must be particularly mindful of the problems adolescent girls face in American culture. They are constantly told through the media that they don't measure up to an unrealistic ideal of physical beauty. Studies clearly show that self-esteem declines when girls reach adolescence, and depression is a common reaction to this.

It is essential that parents not reinforce these social ideals but rather accept their daughters for who they are. Parents must help their teenage daughters discover the best in themselves. They must make their daughters feel loved and valued for the wonderful beings they are. Let them know that they can accomplish much of what they want in life because they are intelligent and competent.

The Business of School

Over the past 10 years, up to a half a million adolescents in the United States dropped out of high school, thus limiting their chances of success in life. Reasons include not liking school, poor grades, having to work, getting in trouble in school, and pregnancy. The typical dropout is two years behind in reading and math by seventh grade, and is likely to have failed one or more school years. Dropouts often end up in low-wage jobs, feeling anger and hostility about their fate. They have a higher rate of depression and drug abuse.

The primary "business" of adolescence is to become educated, therefore parents must be firm and helpful in their effort to see that this goal is accomplished. They must take an active interest in their child's school experiences.

• Be involved in the classes your child takes. Be aware of the future employment options open to your child. Know what is required to graduate and get into college or pursue a particular career.

• Be familiar with the teaching and administrative staff at your child's school. Introduce yourself to your child's counselor. Be cooperative with school personnel.

• Talk to your child about what he or she is learning in school. Pay attention to homework. Talk to your adolescent about his or her assignments, including when they are due. Show an interest in school projects.

• Provide access to books, magazines, newspapers, and reference materials. In today's world access to a computer is essential.

• Always go to "parents' nights" even if your child has excellent grades. It is always helpful to chat with teachers.

• Attend sporting events, plays and any activity your child is involved in. Encourage other family members to attend, too.

• Take adolescents to cultural events and other entertainments that increase their knowledge of subjects they are studying.

A word of caution. Adolescents today work too much. About 75 percent are employed more than 20 hours a week while in high school. Many of them help support their families, others work to buy clothes, ipods, videos and things they want, and some are saving for college. In past generations teens worked informally during the school year—mowing neighbors' lawns, babysitting, helping around the house—and took more structured work during the summer. Informal work allows flexibility in scheduling and freedom to do homework and other important tasks when necessary. Formal employment imposes scheduling limits that often interfere with school requirements and activities. While adolescents develop skills by working—they learn to go on interviews, be on time, get along with co-workers, use cash registers or keyboards, deal with customers, manage money—when they work long hours or at night they are more likely to become exhausted, have a lower resistance to infections, be late for school, sleep in classes, do less homework, get lower grades, have fewer social relationships, miss out on participation in extracurricular school activities, and become stressed and burned out. In some jobs, relationships with adult coworkers increase adolescents' alcohol and drug use.

Parents must pay attention to what their adolescent child does occupationally. Part-time employment is most beneficial if it relates to his or her talents and interests, there are educational benefits, and links to future employment goals. The primary "business" of adolescence is school, therefore, nothing must come before or stand in the way of him or her getting well-educated.

> *My father was a tough guy, an ex-marine, a Goldwater Republican. I was the first hippie in town. He couldn't possibly understand me or me him. The big generation gap between me and my father did get closer. It helped when Springsteen was on the cover of Time and Newsweek. He thought, "Maybe there's something going on here."*
>
> Steven Van Zandt
> Guitarist with Bruce Springsteen's
> E Street Band

Battle Stations

There is a prevailing view in society that adolescence is a time of storm and stress in families but this is not necessarily true. Depending on the attitude of parents there is a broad behavioral range, from families in which discord is rare to families in which there are occasional conflicts, on through to relationships in which conflict and discord are a dominant theme of daily living. The norm appears to be characterized by temporary disturbances rather than continual peace or constant conflict. In fact, the majority of adolescents and their families have healthy relationships and only a small percentage (upwards toward 20 percent) experience severe problems.

As children age, their emotional distance from the family increases as both male and female children spend more time with peers. Fourth graders generally see both mothers and fathers as the most likely source of support; however, as children progress through school, they turn toward same-sex peers for support. From about 10th grade through college, romantic partners became important, which opens the door to possible sexual activity. Interestingly, although adolescents spend more time with peers and away from their families, mothers still rate highly as a major source of support. Adolescents are more likely to seek advice from mothers than fathers; girls more than boys seek advice on personal issues from their mothers.

Far too often discussions with parents are one-sided, with parents explaining their own views rather than trying to understand their adolescent child's perspective. Adolescents rate their conversations with peers as more mutual, allowing for both explaining and understanding. These peer conversations cover topics that include feelings, family life, school issues, personal philosophies, vocational questions, and peer and personal matters. Girls tend to share confidences and offer emotional support in their friendships while boys prefer to share activities, especially sports and games. When it comes to career or college issues, adolescents look to their parents for advice.

Family Tensions

Adolescence is a time when rules and boundaries shift as parents change from being primarily caregivers to primarily counselors. In their new role parents must pick their battles carefully. If you make a major issue out of a son's lateness of 10 minutes, you will lose the chance to have an impact when it comes to more important transgressions. You may have to give in on a daughter's insistence on painting her bedroom purple but put your foot down when she stays on her cell phone until 1 A.M. on a school night in her amethyst sanctuary.

Even in the most loving families there is an increase in family tensions, disagreements, and conflict when children move through adolescence. Adolescents distance themselves from the family in their striving for increased autonomy, which makes interactions with parents seem less warm. Because of normal developmental changes there is a steady and dramatic drop in family time: from 35 percent of waking hours in fifth grade to 14 percent in 12th grade. This can be upsetting to a parent accustomed to having a child participate in family activities such as going to the movies or church or visiting grandparents on Sundays. What can be especially hurtful in a family is the change in sibling relationships as adolescents turn to friends for companionship and emotional support and distance themselves from sisters or brothers.

The way parents handle problems that come up with adolescent children have far-reaching implications. A friend of mine, Pat, told me of an incident that alienated her from her mother. Pat's mother discovered birth control pills in

Pat's bedroom drawer when Pat was 17 and still in high school. The mother drove to the school and waited for Pat to come out. On the way home in the car Pat's mother insisted that Pat tell her who she was having sex with. She then launched into a lecture about morality and sin. Pat told her mother to "mind your own business." The mother and daughter stopped speaking to each other for months. Pat's mother did not attend her daughter's high school graduation.

The Issues

As adolescents physically mature, there tends to be a greater expression of negative feelings by parents, with more disapproval expressed by mothers than fathers. As interpersonal issues become the focus of differences between parents and their adolescent child, disagreements can become quite heated. Many of the quarrels are over day-to-day matters such as chores, privacy, family obligations, bedroom appearance, attitude, dress, hair style, social activities, schoolwork, curfews, friends, money, dating and religious values. More serious conflicts revolve around drinking, drug use and sex.

Dating can be a bone of contention between adolescents and their parents. When early maturing girls date, their partners are generally older, more experienced boys, since these girls are far more developed than boys their own age. It is best to oppose dating until a child is at least 16. Always know the name, address and something about the person your child goes out with.

On a deeper psychological level many common disputes are representative of a natural striving for autonomy and independence on the part of adolescent children. The disagreements serve to create a distance, as the psychological

143

intent of all this bickering leads adolescents into making their own decisions, becoming more responsible, and gaining control over their lives. The desire to separate from parents can be especially stressful for parents who have raised children alone. The adolescent quest for autonomy can make single parents feel abandoned and children feel guilty, a recipe for problems.

It is helpful for parents, single or not, to look at this period as an opportunity to fulfill their own longtime desires. It is time to take that painting class in night school, dine out more with one's mate or friends, get a new puppy. This tells children that it's OK to grow up and look elsewhere for nurturance.

As adolescents separate from the family they turn toward peers for support. Researchers who study adolescent behavior in shopping malls and amusement parks find expressive behaviors such as "touching, smiling, talking, gazing" decrease between mothers and their children as the children reach adolescence, but there is a corresponding increase in these behaviors between peers. Adolescents who remain emotionally close to their parents handle the trials and tribulations of adolescents better those who are not as emotionally attached. Although adolescents often express dissatisfaction with the amount of, speed of, and types of changes that takes place at home, they want their families to be supportive and their home environment peaceful.

Families unable to allow normal separation and growth may provoke behavioral symptoms in their adolescent children, symptoms that include the use of drugs or alcohol, delinquency, or mental illness. The parents of delinquents do not reinforce good behavior and are harsh and punitive when these children misbehave. Often they are not involved in their children's lives. Acting out may be a teen's only way to get parental attention.

At an extreme, there are parents who feel so overwhelmed by their adolescent that they give up responsibility and call in the courts, social service agencies or medical authorities for help. If the conflict becomes intolerable, some adolescents leave home to move in with friends, marry, or simply run away. The expulsion of adolescents from the home can lead to a serious and even permanent family rift and put a child in danger.

Style and Adjustment

Many parents believe that adolescence is a time when less parental influence is needed, but this is not the case. In fact, what is needed is *more* parental influence, but of a different kind. In fact, the greater the parental support for adolescents, the better these children do academically and socially.

There is a clear relationship between a parent's style and an adolescent's adjustment. Researcher Lawrence Steinberg has found that "monitoring, encouragement of achievement, and joint decision making" were highly related to academic achievement, self-reliance, and lower drug usage. Unfortunately, parental involvement with their children generally drops when children reach the teen years. While 75 percent of parents of nine-year-olds claim high or medium involvement in their children's lives, only 55 percent of 14-year-olds say the same.

Supporting children means listening to them without criticism, encouraging their positive aims, showing an interest in their school and outside activities, sharing their companionship, knowing their friends, accepting their style of dress and music, and displaying continued high regard and affection for them. This is a period when parents and their children must solve problems together by looking at options in a rational way. In using induction or logical reasoning with an adolescent a parent is more likely to influence his or her behavior. When disciplining an adolescent it is important that parents explain why a particular rule has been imposed and why breaking that rule is unacceptable. Adolescents must be told how their behavior affects others, and what they must do to remedy misdeeds. Most important, parents must acknowledge and praise the good things their children do.

While teens say they'd welcome complete freedom, they feel safer when there are parental-imposed boundaries around their lives. Parents have to be especially clear about behaviors that are unacceptable. While a degree of rudeness might be tolerated here and there, adolescents should not have the right to insult or otherwise mistreat their parents, siblings or others around them. In imposing limits parents must stay aware of age appropriateness. While a 14-year-old should not be at a party where no parent is in attendance, it's unlikely this rule can be imposed on a 19-year-old, especially if he or she is in college.

Reaching for Adulthood

Unfortunately, too many parents think that punishment and force are the way to get adolescents to behave well. This is because sometimes hitting, slapping, name-calling, nagging and yelling sometimes get children to do what parents want. But what this more often does is stir anger and hostility in children who respond with their own punishment of yelling at and insulting parents. Punitive parents are more likely to have children who develop school problems, behavior problems and who use drugs. These children often become hostile to their parents and other authority figures.

There are specific guidelines for you to follow that will help you prepare your adolescent for adulthood:

• While sometimes it is necessary for parents to make unilateral decisions about their child, particularly when it comes to health or safety issues, most problems can be worked out more easily if the adolescent participates in the decision-making process.

• Remain calm when dealing with an adolescent. It is not helpful for you to emotionally overreact when there is a problem. This doesn't mean not expressing disapproval of a particular behavior, it means confronting issues in a rational way.

• Make a point of knowing your adolescent's friends and also the friend's parents.

• Know where your adolescent is going and who he or she is going with. There should be clear instructions about curfews.

• Do not be too critical. Adolescents need praise for what they do right. Overlook small mistakes or misdeeds. Let children know that grownups make mistakes, too and successes in life often come as a result of errors.

• Pay attention to what your adolescent says. Listen to her opinions without ridicule or sarcasm. Take what she says seriously. Be careful not to invalidate her views and issues.

• Allow your adolescent to test occupational and educational options. Do not be too critical when he changes his mind. Help him to understand his own personality, interests and aptitudes in relationship to the choices he makes.

• Organize family activities that are interesting and age appropriate. Have enjoyable times together.

• Respect privacy. Knock before entering an adolescent's room, and refrain from opening mail, listening in on phone conversations, or reading e-mails. It should be clear to your child that privacy will not be respected if there is evidence of drug or alcohol use in his or her room.

• Assure your adolescent that you are there for him or her. Your relationship should be built on trust and confidence. It should be clear that no matter what the issue—sex, drugs, problem friendships and the like—your child can come to you for help without fear of dreadful consequences.

• Be in attendance and visible at home when your child has a party or get-together. Do not be intrusive unless a problem is sensed. Be sure a parent is home when another adolescent holds a party.

• Never hit, verbally abuse or otherwise mistreat you adolescent. It is harmful to call him names or attack him personality.

• Be alert for problems, be they physical, social or educational. Provide the help needed if the problems warrant professional intervention.

• Have trust and confidence in your adolescent. Suspicions and mistrust are barriers to a good relationship.

• Hug or kiss your adolescent child—often. There is no age limit on needing to feel loved.

It is important that you look at the adolescent stage of development positively. Instead of focusing on what upsets you, concentrate on the good things this time brings. What can be more rewarding than seeing the child you have nurtured for so long come into his or her own as an independent, well-functioning adult?

Big Children, Big Problems

There are things worth battling over with adolescents. At the top of the list is their physical and mental health. There is an endless supply of drugs available to adolescents, including marijuana and cocaine, cigarettes, alcohol, and prescription medications. Thousands of adolescents a year are killed in car accidents, due to excessive drinking. Both female and male adolescents suffer from eating disorders that can lead to their deaths. Feelings of depression or despair are common psychological reactions to the stresses of growing up. Parents must be able to recognize signs that an adolescent is having problems or is engaged in harmful or illegal activities.

The Signs Are There

Adolescents give off clues when they are in psychological trouble. It is up to parents to see what is happening early on so that they can intervene or get professional help. Here are things to look for:

- Severe moodiness and sadness that lasts more than a few days.

- Feelings of worthlessness and hopelessness.

- Lack of interest or concern with people and usual activities.

- A withdrawl from friendships.

- A lack of friendships.

- A lack of energy to do everyday things.

- Excessive complaining and/or crying.

- Excessive focus on illness and health issues.

- Excessive absences from school, and grade failures.

- Lying and/or stealing.

- Lack of interest in appearance.

- Severe weight change, loss or gain.

- Cutting or otherwise injuring self.

• Preoccupation with violence and death.

• Animal cruelty.

• Obsession with guns.

• Unreciprocated romantic obsession.

• Excessive anger and hostility or hate toward others or a particular group.

• Aggression toward others.

• Chronic drunkenness and/or drug use.

• Gang membership.

Ultimate Influences

To truly understand today's adolescents you must acknowledge the tensions they experience. In general, the schools they attend do not meet their intellectual or emotional needs, they are not being provided realistic sex education, national employment policies do not enable enough parental contact and supervision, and they are bombarded by the media with negative images of what they should be. It takes a loving, encouraging and supportive home life for these children to overcome societal obstructions and make a successful transition from childhood into healthy, contented and productive adulthood.

Chapter Eleven
YOU CAN'T TAKE BACK THE WIND

"... as soon as my mother sensed she was pregnant, she knew it would be a girl. She named her Isabel and established a dialogue that continues to the present day. Clinging to the creature developing in her womb, she tried to compensate for the loneliness of a woman who has chosen badly in love. She talked to me aloud, startling everyone who saw her carrying on as if hallucinating, and I suppose that I heard her and answered, although I have no memory of the intrauterine phase of my life."

Isabel Allende
Paula

When I was about eight years old I asked my mother who the most beautiful woman in the world was. She quickly answered, "Eleanor Roosevelt." I rushed to the encyclopedia and eagerly searched for a picture of the great beauty who had become a First Lady. I was astounded to find that Mrs. Roosevelt was a rather plain looking, unfashionable woman. Seeing my puzzlement my mother said, "Read about her and you'll see why she was beautiful." In the years to come I read a lot about Eleanor Roosevelt and was particularly struck by her miserable childhood. Her father was an alcoholic who left the family when Eleanor was very young. Her mother, a true beauty, who died when Eleanor was 10, considered her daughter ugly and gave her a cruel nickname. "If a visitor was there," Eleanor later told friends, "she might turn and say, "She is such a funny child, so old-fashioned, we always call her Granny. I wanted to sink through the floor in shame..." Eleanor Roosevelt, of course, grew up to be a remarkable woman, in a desperate time the eyes and ears of her polio-stricken husband, Franklin. But for all the admiration she received in her lifetime, Eleanor never got over the hurt of being insulted by her mother.

Parents constantly exchange information with their children, some of them even before the children are born. They talk to them directly, and also communicate through gestures, facial expressions, tone of voice and other body signs. Mostly they use language, which can be helpful or harmful. It is important that parents be aware of and understand the impact of the things they say whether it be a joke, a passing criticism, or a direct attack,

A parent's words can make a child feel special and prized. "You are the best thing that ever happened to me." "It was so nice of you to help Aunt Sally today with her food shopping." Or they can be insensitive and hurtful, in a way that damages self-esteem. A friend of mine never forgot her father joking, "Who did your hair, the gardener?" when she came down prom night sporting a somewhat funky hairdo. While my friend's father undoubtedly meant no harm, his carelessness with his words deeply affected his teenage daughter. Once a parent says something unkind to a child, the words can never be taken back, even with an apology.

Straight Talk

A friend of mine told me that she found marijuana and a pipe in her son's room when the boy was 17 and in high school. When she confronted him about it, her son said, "I saw photos of you when you were a '60s hippy. I know you smoked too." My friend explained that she had been in college at the time, the drug was not as potent as it is today, and the laws were not as stringent in the past as they now are. She discussed both the medical and legal consequences of her son's marijuana use. She then took his marijuana and pipe away and told him he was never to bring the stuff in the house again. My friend's husband felt that she should have simply lied to the boy and said no, she never smoked marijuana when she was young, and forbid him to do so. Discussion over.

Parents have to talk to their children about many things, some of them quite serious. How the discussions go depend on the age of the child, the beliefs of the parent, and the kind of relationship the parent and child have. While occasionally it is prudent or discreet to skirt the truth, in general there are principles that promote better communication between a parent and a child.

- It is important that you be as honest as possible, in age-appropriate ways. Obviously you can say more about a situation to an adolescent than you can a young child. You cannot have a close relationship with your children if they don't trust you. Some parents lie to children thinking it's for the children's good. But children usually know or find out they've been lied to and this knowledge not only leads to disillusionment but it teaches children to be dishonest themselves.

- Don't have children lie for you. If you cannot talk on the phone at a particular time, simply say so to a caller or don't answer the phone. Do not have your child say you are not at home when you are standing by his side. If you teach your children to lie for you, they will eventually lie to you.

• "Do as I say and not as I do" does not work. Your children will think you are a hypocrite and ignore your words if they discover you doing something that you forbid them to do. It's hard to convince a teenager not to smoke if you are a pack-a-day smoker yourself.

• Say what you mean and do what you say. If you tell a child you are going to do something, do it. If you have to change a plan or go back on a promise, do not make the change unilaterally, as if you are the only one involved. It's all right to say, "I know I promised to take you bowling this afternoon but I'm far behind on a work project and have to go into the office. How about if we go tomorrow?" This teaches children to be considerate and fair in their own relationships.

• When talking to children, be positive, even when dealing with troublesome situations. If a child gets a failing grade in math it is not the end of the world, rather it's an opportunity to point out that he has done well in his other things and is capable of bringing the math grade up to that standard. Studies show that in happy families there are far more positive interactions made than negative ones, therefore find things to compliment children about. It can be as simple as, "You look very nice today." Children especially like to overhear you speak well of them to others.

• Acknowledge children for the things they do. A simple "thank you" or "that was so kind of you" goes a long way in recognizing good deeds. This tells children that they are appreciated.

• Talk to children about serious things when they are in a position to listen. Your words won't have much effect if your child is running out the door to catch the school bus. Find opportunities to have talks without distractions, be it during car rides, walks, or over lunch in a restaurant.

• Communication should be direct and clear. When a mother announces at the dinner table "I wish someone would straighten up the living room once in a while" the message is indirect, and unlikely to get the desired response. If a father says, "In my day kids weren't so selfish," what is he trying to tell his children? What message are they supposed to get? Is he saying the children are selfish? When communication is vague and unfocused, parents and children cannot adequately share information or solve problems.

• Be polite and respectful when talking to children. Do not command children to do things as if you are a drill sergeant. "Pick up those toys!" "Come here right now!" "Go to bed!" "Take the trash out!" It can lead children to avoid and even ignore a parent who talks this way, and it teaches them to be bossy also.

• Use language to problem-solve. Instead of, "Your room is a mess," try "How can I help you keep your room neat?" ors "What can we do to make it easier for you to put your clothes away?"

• It is not enough to "Just say 'No.'" especially when talking to adolescents. Children are not unthinking robots. They want to know the rationale for things. If you don't want them to take drugs or engage in sex or drink, you must give them good and sensible reasons not to.

Focus on the consequences of their actions, not a trite saying that has little meaning to them.

• As often as possible say "I love you" to your children. Do this especially when they leave the house to go to school and when they go to bed. Nothing makes them feel better about themselves than loving words from their parents.

Attention Must Be Paid

Recently, I walked into the house of an acquaintance at exactly the time she was arguing with her 12-year-old daughter. The mother had taken the girl to a hair salon that day, where a few inches were cut off the daughter's hair. Now the daughter was berating her mother for talking her into getting the haircut. The girl insisted that she looked awful in her shorter hair. The mother responded, "You look fine." and "I think it looks good," to finally a frustrated "You are really annoying me. I don't want to hear about it any more." The daughter stormed upstairs to her room, slamming the bedroom door behind her. The mother yelled up, "You're a brat!"

This is hardly a conversation likely to help an upset child or bring a parent and child together to solve a problem. Instead of insisting that the daughter was wrong in her evaluation of her hair, imagine if the mother had answered, "I see that you're upset. I'm sorry about that. Luckily your hair will grow back to its old length in a few months." This communication would have told the girl her mother was listening, and it would have prevented the conflict.

What children most want from their parents is to be heard. When they express a thought or feeling they want recognition of what they've said. This means listening attentively, understanding the child's point of view, and responding to what the child has said. This is called *active listening*. Children must be able to express their needs, wants and concerns in an atmosphere of acceptance. No thought or idea is silly or stupid, and if there are disagreements or differences of opinion, they are discussed with respect and consideration. There are a number of techniques parents can use to enhance communication with their children.

• When a child talks, give him your undivided attention. With a young child, get down to his level and maintain eye contact with him. Turn off the TV and ignore the telephone if you are having a serious talk with a child. An interruption in a conversation can put an end to the dialogue as he finds something else to do while you are on the phone.

• When it comes to children it is important that you show that you are listening to them. Saying "that's interesting" or "and then what happened?" tells children that you are present in your conversations with them. After you listen, you must respond to what has been said. If a child informs you that her goldfish has died, "I'm sorry about Merlin. I know how much he meant to you," is a better response than, "I'll get you another fish." Also, remember what your child says so you can continue a conversation at another time. This shows you were listening.

• Don't interrupt when a child is speaking. Allow him to finish his thoughts. Do not talk for a child when someone is addressing him. Do not tell children what to say. (I once got on an elevator and a child of about six said hello to me. I asked him what his name was and his mother immediately answered, "James." I said to her, "That's an odd name for a grown woman.")

• Ask open-ended questions that expand a conversation. If a child says, "There's a new girl in my class," in addition to asking her name you might inquire, "What kinds of things do you think you can do to make her feel welcome?" Suppose a child is watching Sesame Street? She says, "I like Grouch." You might ask, "What are the things you like about Grouch?"

• Be patient. It takes some children a long time to put their thoughts into words. Do not interrupt them or hurry them along when they are speaking. Do not correct their word usage or pronunciation during conversations. This breaks their train of thought.

• Act rather than react. Parents sometimes respond to children by yelling before thinking things through. Sometimes they regret what they've said, or have to reverse a decision. It's better to pause a moment before responding, especially if the child is overly emotional. When you are being nagged about something you are not sure about, saying to a child, "Let me think about this a few minutes," is one way to gain some space.

Listening Without Hearing

Parents who have poor communication skills are more likely to employ the silent treatment when angry, avoid eye contact when distressed, watch TV when uninterested, or leave the room when unwilling to work on a problem. Poor communication is the major complaint in families seeking professional help. This is because when conflicts are not openly talked about and faced, resentment builds over time and relationships deteriorate. When family members are unable to negotiate differences, interactions become hurtful and destructive.

The purpose of communication is not to change the mind of the person you are addressing or have your mind changed, but rather to hear all sides of a topic or situation with interest and respect. There is no "winning" when it comes to communication in good relationships, no sense of "giving in" or "giving up." Think about how information is exchanged within your family.

- Are family members respectful and polite when talking to each other?

- Are messages between members clear and direct?

- Are children able to say what they want without being ridiculed, ignored, or otherwise "put down?"

- Do family members say what they mean and present their ideas to the individual to whom they are intended?

- Are people able to stick to the point of a discussion without drifting off to something new or a past grievance?

- Does everyone have an equal opportunity to have his or her say?

- Do people keep their word?

- Are interactions more positive than they are negative?

The Feelings Behind the Words

One Mother's Day, when my son was 12, he handed me a bouquet of pink roses and said, "I'm relieved you made it through another year." I was taken aback by this. I then realized that having lost his father two years earlier, he was telling me how much he worried that I too would die. It occurred to me that he might also be worried about what would happen to him if I weren't around. This one sentence opened up an extended discussion—over cookies and milk—about his fears and concerns.

Often, when children talk, parents must figure out the real meaning behind their words, particularly when it comes to emotional expression. Emotion is the cornerstone of the parent-child relationship. Expressing emotions—anger and fear, sadness and joy, delight and disgust—have important survival benefits in life and yet, all too often, children are educated out of knowing what they are feeling. When they hate something they are told, "it's not nice" to feel this way; when they're afraid they are told, "there's nothing to be frightened of" or "you're being silly." Sad children are told to "put on a happy face" and children in pain are expected to "be brave." This leads to a mixed up sense of ones feelings, to the point that later in life, anger produces guilt, unhappiness is buried, and love becomes a mysterious and often misinterpreted emotion.

161

Psychologist Hiam Ginott believed that when children *feel* right they *behave* right. And what makes them feel right is having parents who accept their feelings. Here are examples of a parent not accepting a child's feelings:

> Child: Mommy, I don't want to get up yet. I'm still tired.
> Parent: You can't be tired. You napped for two hours.
> Child: I am too tired.
> Parent: You're just a little sleepy. Here, put these clothes on and come downstairs.
>
> Child: I hate my teacher.
> Mother: I've met Mr. Smith. He seems to be a very nice man.
> Child: I can't stand him. I think he's a jerk.
> Mother: Don't talk that way about your teacher. It's disrespectful.

Conversing with children is a unique art with rules and meanings of its own. Children are rarely naïve in their communications. Their messages are often in a code that requires deciphering.

Haim Ginott
Between Parent and Child

A Little of This, A Little of That

Educators Elaine Mazlish and Adele Faber have suggested a number of techniques that enhance communication between parents and children and make the relationship between them more peaceful and rewarding. Some of these methods will work with a particular child and others will not; however, in developing better communication skills it is best to encourage cooperation, not confrontation, from your children.

• When a child is emotionally excited or upset, parents sometimes talk too much and intensify the emotional level. Sometimes a couple of words, such as "I see" is enough to show a child you are interested in what she has to say.

• In showing that you are interested, it is effective to reflect a child's feelings back to him or restate what has been said. "I hate my teacher" can be answered with an acknowledgement of "You are upset with Mr. Smith." When a child knows that a parent has heard him, he is likely to continue talking about a situation.

• Help your child know what she is feeling by mirroring back the emotions she displays. If a child says, "Susie is having a party and I'm not invited," the answer is not, "When you have a party, don't invite her," but rather, "You sound disappointed that you haven't been invited." This technique helps children understand what they are really feeling, thus making communication and problem-solving easier for them.

• It sometimes helps to give a child what he or she wants in fantasy. If a child complains, "Everybody in the class has been to Disneyworld except me," instead of answering, "I doubt everyone has gone there," let the child have the thing he desires another way. "I wish I could take you there this very afternoon." If your daughter wants go out on a date but she is too young, try, "I hope you have a lot of fun in two years when you have your first date."

• It's easier for children to solve a problem if it is clearly described to them. By saying, "Would you please close the refrigerator door," a parent is nonconfrontive while informing a child that he or she has to do something. "You always leave the refrigerator door open," blames a child for having done something in the past. Give your child information instead of insulting or blaming him; this is always more helpful in accomplishing a goal. And often, the less said, the better. "Here's your lunch!" works better than, "You're forgetting your lunch again." And forget the sarcasm. "If your head wasn't attached to your shoulders you'd probably forget that, too." Not necessary.

• You can express honest feelings without attacking your child. "I get annoyed when you take my hairbrush out of my bathroom" is more effective than, "You're always taking things that don't belong to you." "I don't like having to pick your towel off of the bathroom floor after you take a shower," is better than, "You are really inconsiderate when you drop your towel wherever you want."

• Sometimes a written note works, especially if done in good spirit. A note saying, "I'd like you to tidy your room up after school today, pal. Thanks, Dad. Have a good day," encourages rather than commands.

Quiet Down

It is easy to close down communication with a child. Often parents think they are engaged in a dialogue when, in fact, the child has tuned them out. Here are things parents should avoid doing if they want open and honest conversations with their children.

• Refrain from using ridicule or making harsh judgments that make a child feel badly about herself. "You will never get into college with those grades!" "Is there anyone in the class who did worse on that exam?" These kinds of comments are not designed to help a child do better.

• Do not name-call. "How dumb can you be to get this grade in math?" "You are such a bird brain." Be careful of nicknames you or others give your child. "Bozo" "Stinky" "Fat Albert" "Four Eyes" are cruel, not funny. Names do hurt children, and the hurt can last a lifetime.

• The blame-game makes children feel guilty rather than cooperative. "This is the second barrette you've lost. How can you be so careless?" Wouldn't it be kinder to say, "I'm sorry you lost your favorite barrette?" and leave it at that?

• Threats and warnings rarely work. "Do that again and you'll be sorry." "Put your jacket on or you'll catch a cold." After a while children ignore a parent who continually cautions them about future events. Even if a child complies because of threats, he or she tends to tune the parent out after a while.

• Lecturing and moralizing turns children off. "Imagine what people would think of you if they knew how late you stayed out." "When I was your age I never would have embarrassed my parents by doing this."

• Comparisons make children angry. "Your sister never once got a failing grade." "I'll bet none of your friends talk to their parents this way." Whether they say so or not, children in this situation are thinking of what they wish they could answer. "I could care less what my sister did in school." "How would you know what my friends do in their own homes?"

• Martyrdom makes children feel guilty, which can lead them to withdraw from a relationship with a parent. "I work two jobs to put a roof over your head." "You are driving me crazy." "Do you know what I sacrificed to give you music lessons and now you talk to me that way?" It's difficult for children to admire a parent who plays the victim role.

• Do not yell. While you may frighten your children with your loudness, it pushes them away from you emotionally. This also teaches them to holler when they are upset.

Meeting In the Middle

There is no family that doesn't have problems or disagreements. Communicating about them is a first step in facing these issues or settling disputes. One way for parents and children to resolve conflicts is to have family meetings, in which everyone gets to have their say. Here are guidelines to make it easier to come together in a way that meets everyone's needs.

• Choose a time that is convenient for everyone to have a meeting. All persons involved in an issue must attend.

• Agree to respect each other. Parents and children should express their points of view without being attacked or ridiculed.

• Define the problem. Be sure everyone agrees it is fairly stated. "We are all gaining too much weight." "Your school grades are not what we want them to be." "I want us to get cable TV."

• Identify goals everyone has in common. "We want to switch to a healthier diet." "School grades must come up."

• Express feelings honestly, and clarify with feedback. "I think you kids watch too much TV as it is." "It sounds as if you're saying you don't want to go to church anymore."

• Stick to the issue being discussed. Don't get sidetracked by bringing up past mistakes or behaviors. Do not allow the subject to be changed, as in, "I wasn't happy with your grades last year either."

• Brainstorm possible solutions. Come up with at least three alternatives. Evaluate the alternatives together. Decide which one to try. "How about if I go to church only on important holidays?" "Let's do a healthy shopping list on Sundays and stick to this when we go grocery shopping on Monday." "We'll get cable TV but limit TV use to two hours a day, after homework is completed."

• Set a date for the next family meeting, when the outcome of decisions made will be evaluated.

Regrets Are a Part of Life

In the course of any relationship people occasionally say things they wish they hadn't. Children particularly have long memories when they feel mistreated or their feelings are hurt. Parents are human and as such they make mistakes. It is OK to say to a child "I am sorry" if you do or say something that you regret. This teaches children to apologize also when they feel they have done something wrong.

> *I seek your forgiveness for all the times I talked when I should have listened; got angry when I should have been patient; acted when I should have waited; feared when I should have delighted; scolded when I should have encouraged; criticized when I should have complimented; said no when I should have said yes and said yes when I should have said no....Most of all, I am sorry for all the times I did not affirm all the wonderful things you are and did that got lost in parental admonitions about things left undone or thought not well enough done...*
>
> Miriam Wright Edelman
> *The Measure of Our Success*

Chapter Twelve
TEACHING CHILDREN WELL

And I just lost my mind. I thought I might begin smashing things, including Sam. I shouted at the top of my lungs...and grabbed him by his pipe-cleaner arm and jerked him in the direction of his room, where he spent the next ten minutes crying bitter tears. It's so awful, attacking your child. It is the worst thing I know...I did what all good parents do: calmed down enough to go apologize, and beg for his forgiveness while simultaneously expressing a deep concern about his disappointing character. He said I was the meanest person on earth next to Darth Vader.

Anne Lamott
Traveling Mercies

I recently attended a dinner party during which a few of the guests discussed their childhoods. The subject of discipline came up. One woman recounted an incident when she was in her teens when she and a couple of girlfriends were watching a movie and the lead actress in the film appeared very sophisticated by drinking a martini. In a desire to imitate the actress, the girls poured themselves drinks from a bottle of vodka the woman's father had in a kitchen cabinet. They replaced the vodka they drank with water. It took only one thin martini for the father to discover what his daughter and her friends had done. He immediately grounded his daughter and forbid her to go out of the house for a month for anything other than school. I asked the woman if this put an end to her drinking with her girlfriends. She laughed and said, "Are you kidding? Absolutely not!" She added that she made sure she never again got caught.

A prime responsibility of parents is to teach their children to behave in socially acceptable and appropriate ways—at home, school, and in the community—and develop the self-control needed to get along with others and accomplish important life tasks. Parents want their children to be responsible, trustworthy, competent, helpful, considerate and caring human beings, behaviors considered prosocial. In attempting to mold the behavior of their children parents try various techniques and methods, which they refer to as discipline. Almost half of all interactions parents have with children after the age of two focus on regulating behavior. What is particularly interesting about these efforts is how frequently they fail to bring about the behavior parents want to instill.

Good and Not So Good Behavior

I once grew clematis on the porch of my house. Every year for 10 years I fed it plant food and carefully pruned it and watched delightfully as it wrapped itself around a pillar each spring and summer and spread its pink flowers across the porch. One day I went out to the porch to tend the plant and discovered it piled at the base of the pillar, demolished by my four-year-old who, pruning shears in hand, had decided to "help Mommy" by "fixing the tree." I was both flabbergasted and devastated and so angry I yelled at him. When I calmed down I realized that my son's gardening exercise was an attempt to make me happy. The "badness" of his behavior was in my mind alone. I apologized to my upset child and thanked him for his effort to help me with my gardening. (I was heartbroken over my poor clematis for years but kept this to myself.)

The "goodness" or "badness" of a child's behavior often rests outside himself or herself. Children aren't thinking, "I'm acting wrong" when they do things their parents disapprove of. They are simply doing what they want to do to satisfy a need, be it to be loved, express anger, obtain something, get revenge, relieve boredom, be creative or gain a feeling of competency. These are exactly the same reasons parents do things. A child picks up a treasured painted vase because she wants to look at it. One parent decides this is a behavior that requires a scolding, another takes the vase away from the child and puts it up high, and a third holds the vase with the child and points out the pretty flowers on it.

As a parent you must think about why a child is doing something before reacting to the action. What you will usually find is that what you are calling "bad" or misbehavior is basically your wanting your needs to be met over you child wanting her needs to be met. You want quiet when your child wants to chase the dog around the living room. You want to talk to a friend on the phone when your child wants to talk to you. You want the house to be tidy when your child wants to spread his CD collection across the dining room table. Whether a behavior is considered "good" or "bad" depends on your own mood or circumstances. On a day when you are relaxed and rested, you laugh at the interaction between your child and her dog. On a day that you have a report to finish for your job, the kid and dog get on your nerves and you yell at them to settle down.

This is not to say that there are not behaviors that are clearly unacceptable. Disrespectful or hurtful actions or words directed toward others, a refusal to cooperate at important times, and posing a danger to another person or himself are pretty high on the list of what must be addressed and changed. Even so, there is an emotional motive behind inappropriate actions, and it is this cause that must be understood if a parent is to teach a child right from wrong.

Confusing Discipline and Punishment

Do not confuse discipline with punishment. They are not the same thing—and the results are not the same. From its old French root, the word *discipline* comes from disciple, or student; it means instruction or knowledge. The object of discipline, then, is to teach something. It is about guidance and cooperation in the learning process. The intent is to have children internalize "good" behavior, that is, have inner controls concerning what they do. Specifically, the goal is to have children behave appropriately even when parents are not around.

When I talk to parents about their discipline practices I find that their methods include criticizing their children, withholding an allowance, bribing them, pinching them, calling them names, instilling guilt, isolating them, revoking their privileges, withholding food, grounding them, shaming them, isolating them, ignoring them and hitting them. These actions are not about discipline, they are punishments. Their intent is to change, shape or mold behavior through punitive measures. The principle behind punishment rests on the belief that if a particular act results in discomfort, the act is unlikely to be repeated. Theoretically, grounding a child for having a martini should put an end to this kind of behavior. And yet, if this method of teaching worked, parents would not have to repeatedly penalize children for the same behavior. My dinner companion would no longer drink martinis when her father wasn't around.

It is not uncommon for parents to withdraw their love and affection as a way to influence their child's behavior. They disapprove of him, ignore him or resort to "the silent treatment." These are forms of punishment that, instead of teaching a child something, make him feel awful about himself, as if he is a non-person. The anxiety this method produces tends to change behavior temporarily, but again, the child does not internalize parental desires. Furthermore, feelings of being unloved may backfire as the child seeks affection and approval outside the home or acts out in attention-getting ways.

Punishment can, of course, lead children to behave as parents desire, but this is because of fear of the consequences rather than because they believe it is important to uphold a particular parental value. You want your child to follow certain rules because they are right, not because he or she is afraid of you.

The Problem With Punishment

Studies in psychology have shown that to be effective, a punishment must be administered immediately after a misbehavior. Because parents are not always around when children do things they've been told not to, there is a delay between the act and the penalty, making the penalty ineffective. Also, punishment must be consistent, which means the same misbehavior must always be punished. Parents are busy, or tired, or in a good or bad mood on a particular day, causing a specific behavior to be penalized one day but ignored the next.

What often makes punishment ineffective is that the penalty usually has nothing to do with the misdeed.

173

To punish a failing grade on a history exam by keeping a child from a sleepover at a friend's house a week later doesn't address the reason for the failure. To really be effective, an alternative to an undesired behavior must be offered. It doesn't do much good to send a child to her room for misbehaving at dinner if she is not told what is expected of her when she returns to the table.

Punishment often leads to the suppression of a behavior but not the stopping of it. Scolding a child for getting into the cookie jar might keep her out of it for a little while, but as soon as possible she will be in search of a cookie treat again. Revoking a privilege for staying out past his curfew may lead a teenager to sleep at a friend's house when he wants to stay out late. In an effort to avoid punishment, older children avoid a punishing parent.

Punishment can lead to unfortunate emotional reactions. Think of what it is like for a young child to be insulted, yelled at or spanked by the person he has come to rely on for his well being, the parent who is supposed to be loving and trustworthy? There is considerable evidence that stress in early childhood causes structural and chemical changes in areas of the brain involved in emotional development. In growing up, children who have been traumatized by harsh punishment can develop symptoms of post-traumatic stress, including anxiety, depression and suicidal thoughts. Depression is presently the major mental health problem in adolescents and college students and at its root is a sense of helplessness and hopelessness that comes from parental over-control. Studies of long- term life satisfaction show that feelings of powerlessness are instrumental in making people unhappy.

Some children are so intimated by parents who rely on power to mold behavior they become passive and compliant, which has negative implications when it comes to succeeding in life. Other children resist punitive parents and become angry, defiant, rebellious and in extreme cases violent and anti-social.

The most severe effects of strong punishment are the hostility and anger it provokes. Anyone who has been harshly reprimanded by a teacher or employer can attest to the feeling of resentment that results; this is the same feeling experienced by children in similar situations. When children are unable to express their feelings about being treated this way for fear of greater punishment, they may become passive-aggressive, a getting-back at parents with behaviors such as procrastination, pouting, inattentiveness, stubbornness or inefficiency.

Ironically, punishment can have the opposite effect of what is intended. If a child views his or her punishment as unfair or unreasonable, the child may become angry and resentful to the point of ignoring continued threats. Parental control in such situations is lessened.

In some cases, a punishment is worth the price a child has to pay for it. If a child gets little notice from parents for "good" behavior, he might write on a wall, hit a sibling or otherwise engage in attention-getting behavior. A parent's angry response might be a satisfying experience, one that leads to a repetition of the behavior.

Parents who rely on punishment to mold behavior often lose control over their children and their influence is diminished, especially when adolescence hits. Teenagers who feel oppressed stay out of the house, except to eat and sleep. Some run away from home to get away from punitive parents, putting themselves at risk on the street. It is not uncommon for parents to kick their teenage children out of the house, calling them "incorrigible," "uncontrollable," or "rebellious." These parents would rather lose their children than lose their power over them.

Hitting and Spanking As Discipline Methods

It is a sad but true fact that the majority of parents in America use physical force in an effort to control or correct their children's behavior. Using their hands or an object such as a belt (or pot, or telephone wire, or cane or dog leash, as my students report), they are determined to whack children into behaving well. A national study found that 35 percent of parents slapped the hands of their infant, and 94 percent hit their three–four-year-old children. Half of these parents continued to hit their children until they were 12, a third were hitting their 14-year-olds, and 13 percent were still at it when the children turned 17. This is occurring at a time when many nations, including Sweden, Germany, Italy, Israel, and Denmark have outlawed these assaults on children.

OK, I'll say it loud and clear: Don't hit or spank your children. First, because it's unkind; second, because it's unnecessary; and third, because it leads to far greater problems than the behavior that led to this painful punishment.

Why do parents hit their children? Primarily because they were taught to treat children this way—by their own parents, because of religious teachings, and because they don't know another way to discipline. Most parents who hit their children were themselves hit as children (although many who were hit or spanked do not do this), and they are being loyal to the parents who mistreated them by insisting, "I got hit, and I turned out fine." My response to this is, how do you know you wouldn't have turned out as good or better if your parents had used more humane methods of behavior regulation? It is painful for any person who has been hit or spanked in childhood to face into this mistreatment and see it for what it was—violence against a child. This blindness to their childhood reality keeps many parents from changing their views about hitting or spanking.

While most parents who hit or spank their children do not intend to do injury, they nevertheless can cause both physical and psychological problems that last a lifetime.

- *Betrayal of trust.* It is essential that children develop trust in the world and a sense that things will be all right for them in it. They particularly look to parents to keep them safe and out of harm's way. Their trust in the world and the people around them can become impaired when they are hit or spanked by the person who is supposed to be the most reliable in their lives. Although a child will stay attached and even love a parent who mistreats her, a part of her comes to see that parent as a danger. A child counts on her parents to always act in her best interest. Self-confidence and self-esteem are damaged when a child realizes that the person she most relies on has not protected her from harm.

- *Psychological trauma.* Any number of psychological disorders can result from being hit or spanked. Children feel humiliated and worthless when treated badly, feelings that lead to anxiety and depression. These feelings in turn interfere with school success and social adjustment.

In the long run, if psychologically-damaged children become school dropouts or delinquents, society at large suffers. The desire to still the pain of being mistreated leads some children into the excessive use of drugs or alcohol.

• *Sexual implications*. Children must be taught to respect their bodies and view them pleasurably. When children are hit or spanked, particularly on the buttocks, their bodies are no longer their own. Later in life, their sexual behaviors may be reflective of this perception.

• *Might makes right*. Hitting and spanking children tells children that force is an acceptable way to deal with people. The child who learns about power persuasion can become the class bully. In adulthood, he or she may be a wife or husband abuser. In the workplace, as an employer, he can be a tyrant to those who work under him. Abuse against elderly parents who in the past hit or spanked their children is not an uncommon phenomenon in our society.

• *Anger and aggression*. Children become angry and resentful when they are mistreated, and they tend to imitate their parent's actions when at odds with others. In one disturbing study it was found that 100 percent of children who were physically punished went on to severely assault a brother or sister. Of children who were not physically punished, 20 percent injured a sibling. As adults, aggressive and assaultive children are likely to find themselves in legal trouble. Spanking and hitting children in no small measure is responsible for the nation's high prison incarceration rates. Sometimes anger can be displaced, and instead of facing into punitive parents, children vent their rage on animals, and adults strike out against political or social groups they disagree with.

• *Physical injury.* Accidents happen, particularly when a parent is angry enough to hit a child. Brain damage can result from shaking a young child; hitting a child's hands, arms or legs can cause nerve damage or fractures; smacking a child in the face can lead to an eye injury; a blow to the buttocks can cause kidney damage. When a weapon such as a belt is used the chance of serious injury increases. A parent who hits or spanks a child is usually feeling frustrated or angry. Such emotional states are a recipe for doing grave harm. In some cases, injuries as a result of being hit or spanked become apparent to family members, friends or school officials, and lead to intervention by legal authorities.

• *Interpersonal relationships.* Hitting or spanking a child can set him or her up for a difficult adult life. What does a father hitting a daughter tell her about men? That it's OK for a man who is supposed to love her to also mistreat her? And a mother hitting a son? How can this not affect the son's relationships with women? A child who is hit or spanked by a parent feels rejected, and this feeling leads adult men and women into relationships that reinforce these negative feelings. People who suffer in childhood at the hands of their parents are more likely to be victimized in adulthood than those who have been treated with love and respect.

• *Lack of compassion.* To live well in the world a person must care about others, come out of himself and have the ability to put himself in another's place. Parents who hit their children display an inability to feel what their children are feeling. This lack of empathy is transmitted to children, who go out in the world deficient in the kind of compassion needed to connect well with others and live a happy and peaceful life.

If you were hit or spanked when growing up it is easy to revert to these techniques when feeling annoyed at your children. While it is true that many people so treated live loving and caring lives, and many children disciplined in this same fashion seem to thrive, when you feel you are about to spank your child, think of the words I once heard a researcher in child development say, "If you hit your children and they turn out alright, you weren't a good parent—you were lucky."

Violence to children produces a violent and ill society. True authority dismisses humiliation. Its discipline is based on listening and talking, on trust, respect and protection of the weaker. It gives children the assistance they need to become responsible adults who will not turn to vengeful actions such as wars and dictatorships. They will simply return to others what they once received and what they learned by example: protection and respect.

Alice Miller
An Open Letter To All Responsible Politicians

Discipline As Problem Solving

It has been said that the only way to solve a problem is to solve a problem. This is basically what discipline is supposed to do. Your five-year-old gets out of bed in the middle of the night and wanders around the house. Your teenage daughter insists on getting a tattoo and you are opposed to it. Your ten-year-old does not do her homework. These are problems that warrant solutions. You have to come up with a method of discipline that solves these problems in a non-threatening way. Teaching a child to behave well is a team effort, and since the child is half the team it works well to enlist his or her help in solving problems in positive ways.

The object of discipline is to help children understand the behavior expectations parents have for them. These expectations must be reasonable and appropriate in light of a child's age, personality and abilities. A two-year-old will not "be quiet" when Mommy is on the phone. An active six-year-old has a lot of trouble "sitting still."

There is no one best method for you to use to teach a child to behave in responsible ways or turn her away from undesirable behavior. The method you choose depends on many factors, including the age and personality of your child, your emotional state, the particular problem being addressed, and your life circumstances. The same technique will not work when trying to keep your toddler from having a temper tantrum in the supermarket and your adolescent from coming home by curfew. Because so many different problems and issues arise in the course of raising a child it is important that you have an arsenal of discipline methods at your disposal, and an ability to change direction when one doesn't work or circumstances change. In the end, how influential you are in teaching your child what you want her to know depends in large part upon the relationship you have with her over the years. You can't instill your own values and beliefs if your child has no confidence that you have her best interests at heart and not your own. If you have a hostile relationship with your child and there are negative feelings between you, it is much harder to teach him or her anything. It is an uphill battle until you get the help you need to make your relationship with your child a loving and positive one.

> *... as a society we are employing the wrong strategies to reduce the self-destructive and socially unacceptable behaviors of young people that occur with shocking frequency—alcoholism, smoking, drug abuse, delinquent activities, dropping out of school, drunk driving, vandalism and other forms of violence, premarital pregnancies, rape, suicide. The ever-increasing frequency of these behaviors is certainly sufficient evidence that the way we have traditionally disciplined children at home and in our schools has not worked. In fact, discipling children the way we do may be more a cause than a cure for these unwanted behaviors.*
>
> Thomas Gordon
> *Discipline That Works*

First Things First

You can't solve a problem until you identify it. You must find out what the child needs. You are in a department store and your five-year-old child is whining. A child doesn't fuss without a reason. Is he hungry? Tired? Bored? Your teenager is argumentative all day and then slams her bedroom door with a loud bang. Did she have an argument with a friend? Is she going through hormonal changes? Is she feeling pressured by schoolwork? Is she about to leave for college and bickering is her way of emotionally separating from her parents so that the impending actual separation is more tolerable?

When an infant cries or fusses, you must use a process of elimination to determine what he needs. See if he's wet. Try to feed him. Does he need to be burped? Does he need to be held? It's easier with older children. Simply ask them what the problem is. "What's upsetting you today?" "Why are you not dressed for school?" "What do you want?"

Once a problem is identified you must consider solutions. If your child is fussing in a department store you have a number of options: You can leave the department store and go home; you can stop at the mall food court and get something to eat; you can stop in a bookstore and have your child pick out something he'd like to read with you. It is best to enlist a child's help in solving the problem. "Does your tummy feel like it needs something to eat? What would your tummy like to eat?" "If you need a rest, let me know." "What can we do to help you get to school on time?" Whatever you choose will hopefully solve the problem, but sometimes it doesn't. Move on to another possible solution.

Preventing Problems

I recently had a conversation with a woman who talked about her two-year-old's desire to touch objects of art that the woman had sprinkled around her house. She asked me how she could stop her child from doing this. I gave her a simple solution: move the objects out of the child's reach. The woman didn't like my suggestion. She insisted that the child should learn to respect her mother's things. She had no intention of rearranging her home for a toddler's sake. It occurred to me to tell this self-absorbed mother that if she wasn't willing to move a picture frame out of the way to avoid problems with her little one, perhaps she wasn't ready to have kids.

It seems so sensible to avoid problems with children before they occur. Why stir the pot of discord if it isn't necessary?

One way to avoid problems with young children is to childproof your home. This means blocking off dangerous areas such as the top of a staircase, locking cabinets that hold medications, fencing off areas around the house that could prove harmful, and putting valuables and dangerous items out of reach. Once this is done you can teach children that certain rooms or things are off limits. Simply communicate to a child that "I don't want you to go into the laundry room" or "Please don't bother the dog while she's eating." You may have to tell a child these things a few times but eventually she will understand and comply. You can reinforce this behavior with "Lucy is happy you didn't go near her food bowl today" or "Thank you for staying out of my office."

Another way to prevent a problem is to tell a child what is expected of her when she is in a restaurant, super-market, friend's house or anywhere else. Prepare her for what she will do and see. "When we go to the supermarket today you'll be in charge of getting the cereal. We don't make a lot of noise or run in the supermarket. You must stay with Daddy. I'm so glad you're going to be there to help me." Restaurant visits can be potentially troublesome because young children tend to get bored and restless while waiting for food. If you take along crayons and paper, a puzzle, or a book to read you can have a more enjoyable time. On long car trips take toys, stuffed animals, books and, if possible, videos. Also take snacks with you when you go on an outing—crackers, fruit, raisins, juice. There are few things crankier than a hungry child.

When possible, practice appropriate behavior. Run through scenarios with your child. "What are we going to do when we go to a restaurant for lunch?" "When we visit grandma in the hospital we have to be very quiet. Can you show me how to be very quiet?" It is important that children are clear about what is expected of them.

An especially good way to avoid problems is to modify a child's environment. If you want your child to calm down before bedtime, turn off the TV, dim the lights and read him a story. Provide coloring books and puzzles and other interesting things if you want to keep a child from reaching for things you don't want him to have. If your teenage daughter's room is a mess and she never hangs her clothes up, work with her to come up with easy storage solutions, be it a line of colorful crates or a wall of shelving. Sometimes it is helpful to change the environment altogether. A child who insists on bouncing a ball in the house can be directed outside and allowed to toss the ball against a wall.

Forewarn your child when you are about to change his routine. "Sweetie, bath time in 15 minutes." Or, "I'm making dinner. We're going to eat very soon, so after your program is over, please wash your hands." This gives a child time to adjust and makes him more cooperative. You can give this warning a few times. "OK, we're down to 10 minutes."

When you involve your child in decision-making, he tends to be more cooperative. Giving him choices, rather than telling them what to do, is a helpful technique. "Do you want to wear your red shirt or your yellow one to day care today?" "We are going to the store in a little while. Do you want to walk next to Daddy or ride in the cart?" Let him choose the book he wants read at night. This technique can work in almost any instance. It gives a child a sense of autonomy and a feeling of competence.

Offering a substitute activity for one that is undesirable often works well. Instead of saying, "No, don't touch that," focus your child's attention on something else. A toy telephone can replace a young child's reach for a parent's cell phone. A puzzle can be substituted for pulling things out of drawers. Children like to be busy; therefore, you must give them things to do that will hold their interest.

Do not be too critical when a child makes mistakes. Let him try things. You can make suggestions that will help but do not take over a task when your child gets frustrated. It's not the end of the world if a shirt and pants don't match. Children break things from time to time. Patience and understanding are needed if problems with children are to be avoided.

Discipline Without Conflict

For a number of years my teenage son wore a tattered cap I hated. I repeatedly told him how much it annoyed me when he left the house in that cap. "It's on my head, Mom, not yours" was his frequent reply. Nothing I said was going to get that hat off of his head.

In every parent-child relationship there is tension and disagreement from time to time. This is because children, if they are not punished into passivity, challenge their parents'

186

beliefs and rules in seeking independence as they grow. In young children there will be conflicts about food and bedtime; in older children the list grows to clothes, friendships, sex, schoolwork, money, religious attitudes, and sometimes smoking and drinking.

If you go head to head with a child in an effort to control your child and "win" an argument—by nagging, yelling, threatening or punishing—you may force your child to do things your way. But often the change is temporary, and it comes with resentment and anger. If your child "wins" her way - by whining, crying or having temper tantrums—you will feel frustrated and ineffectual as a parent and your child will learn that her needs are more important than anyone else's and if she fusses enough she can get her way. Your goal is to resolve conflicts in a "no-win, no-lose" way, whereby both you and your child come to agreements over issues of concern. In essence, you and your child cooperate in the discipline process. A child who has a voice in solving a problem is more likely to accept a decision concerning the problem than one who has a solution forced upon him.

Resolving conflicts with a child entails defining the problem and having both parent and child come up with possible solutions. In the case of my son and his hat, we agreed that he would wear the ratty cap when he went to school or was out with his friends. He'd leave the cap home when there were family outings.

It is not always easy to come up with solutions when there is conflict with a child but most issues can be resolved—with patience. Your 16-year-old daughter wants to go to a party at the house of a friend of a friend, someone you do not know. You do not want her at the home of a stranger.

Your daughter insists on going. You offer to drive her and come in and meet the friend's friend's parents. Your daughter says absolutely not; this would be too embarrassing. Finally the two of you decide that you will call the friend's friend's parents to make sure they will be home during the party and that alcohol will not be served. You also agree on a curfew for leaving the party.

Techniques to Avoid

Physical mistreatment: hitting, slapping, pinching, punching or otherwise attacking children produces angry, hostile children rather than cooperative and responsible ones.

Yelling: This common practice allows parents to vent their anger and frustration but to children this is just a lot of noise that makes them anxious and likely to tune parents out.

Threats: Intimidating a child with words like, "You are going to be one sorry young man," or "I better not catch you out of bed," may enable a parent to get his or her way, but the child becomes angry and resentful.

Shaming: It is hurtful to a child to belittle him with comments such as "You are acting like a baby," or "How dumb can you be?"

Nagging: It is irritating to children to be told to do something over and over again. And it makes a parent angry to have to repeat a request many times.

Lecturing: Children are not interested in their parents' speeches about education, smoking, drugs, friendships or anything else parents have opinions on. They tend to ignore advice that begins with "When I was young..." or "If I were you I would ..."

Instilling guilt: Children should not be made to feel overly responsible for things that go wrong. Statements such as, "Do you know how hard I worked to buy you that dress and now you've ruined it," only serve to make a child feel badly about herself.

Traps: If you have something to discuss, discuss it. Do not set up your child to get caught lying about misbehavior. It is dishonest to say, "How did you do in the math exam?" after the math teacher has called you to talk about your child's poor grade.

Setting Limits

Children need rules and regulations, guidelines telling them what is expected of them behaviorally and what is unacceptable. There are rules about dinnertime, bedtime, homework, phone use, the use of the family car, household chores, money, curfew, and many other every day issues that have a potential for conflict.

- When your children are young, rules should be simple to understand, as in, "You must brush your teeth before bedtime." Older children, particularly adolescents, need justification for rules. "The legal curfew in this township is midnight and that's the time you have to be in."

• When setting limits on behavior, do so in a respectful way. "You can make ice cream sundaes but I expect you to clean up any mess you make."

• Children must be reminded frequently of rules. Just about every time my teenage son went out at night I said, "Be sure to call me if you're going to be late so that I don't worry." It annoyed him after a while but I said it anyway. I eventually shortened the rule to "Call me," because it was clear what I meant.

• Rules must be fair, reasonable and consistent. I know a parent who imposes an unrealistic 9 P.M. weekend curfew on her teenage daughter, which the daughter never complies with. If you are not sure about what is appropriate at a particular age, talk to other parents or teachers. When rules do not make sense, children cannot adhere to them. A child can have a regular bedtime and be sent to her room at this time, but she cannot be forced to fall asleep no matter what a parent wants.

• Rules must be applied equally in families or children will recognize the hypocrisy of seeing them defied by some. It is difficult for a parent to defend a rule that he or she ignores. A parent who smokes will have an impossible time forbidding her teenager to smoke. A single or divorced parent who allows a date to "sleep over" will have an uphill battle trying to regulate his or her children's sexual conduct.

• There are times when the rules must be bent. Why deny your nine-year-old sports fanatic child a chance to watch his city's team play a championship game on TV because it lasts past his usual bedtime? It may be a once in a lifetime event.

• Children are most likely to follow rules if they are involved in making them. When possible, include your child in making such decisions. A bedtime can be negotiated, children can have a say in what TV shows they are allowed to watch, and there can be input on when homework is to be done. Participating in rule-making makes children more responsible than if only parents control rules.

When rules are fair, reasonable and consistent, children internalize parental values. By the time they are adolescents they will adhere to most of them without prodding.

Admiration and Encouragement

Children love to be loved. They want to get their parents' attention and have their parents be proud of them. Too often parents focus on the behaviors they don't want and forget to emphasize and reinforce the behaviors they approve of. It is easy to criticize a child when he does things you don't approve of but it is more helpful to encourage him to do his best. Learn to use words that support his efforts. "I know that you can bring that grade up." "Make nice to the doggy. Very good. I think the doggy is very happy to know you."

When you praise a child, be specific. Rather than "good job," or "you're a great kid" tell the child what he has done right. "I'm so happy you got an A in that report. I know how hard you worked on it." "You did a good job tidying your room." Do not give backhanded compliments such as, "I like the way you made your bed. I wish you did it like that every day."

191

Train yourself to give your child attention for the good things he does. Show an interest in his activities. "I liked the way you handled that problem." "It was a lot of fun watching you play ball today." "Thanks for washing the car. It looks great." "You're doing so much better on the guitar. I really enjoyed listening to that song. "

Using "I" Messages

When children do things parents don't approve of, parents have a tendency to criticize them, assign blame and even ridicule them. These are called "you-messages." Here is a sample:

"You are being rude to your sister."
"Your room is a mess."
"You should be ashamed of yourself."
"How could you be so careless?"
"You are a bad boy."

When you accuse a child of something, his instinct is to defend himself and strike back. "She was rude to me first." "I have too much homework to do to worry about my room." By using "I-messages" you change the dynamics of the problem by telling your child why you have a problem with his behavior, and enlisting his help in making changes. Notice the difference between saying, "You're driving me crazy. Lower that stereo," and, "I can't talk to grandma on the phone when you're playing your music so loudly. Please turn it down." Children are more likely to change their behavior when they don't feel judged. An "I-message" changes, "You keep leaving your dirty clothes on the floor" to the less accusatory, "I have a hard time bending over to pick up your clothes. It really bothers me to have to do this."

"I- messages" are effective when praising or encouraging children. "I really appreciate you doing the dishes tonight." "It made my day to see your grade on the math test." It always makes children feel good to know they are appreciated.

Plain Speaking

It is not uncommon for parents to get into debates and arguments with children over chores, homework, privileges and other day-to-day things. The arguments often turn unpleasant and rarely accomplish what a parent intends. Often parents are not clear and concise when they talk to their children. This leaves the door open for children to disagree, get angry and often ignore what is being said. Parents often say pointless things like "Your room looks like World War III" in an attempt to get their children to tidy a bedroom. When this is not accomplished they move to the more obvious, "Your room is a mess." Sometimes they even beg. "Will you please clean up this room?" Finally they threaten, "If this room is not clean by dinnertime you can't go out with your friends this weekend."

Try a calm, direct approach, stick to the point, and don't get into debates, arguments or discussions. Try a technique known as "the broken record," a continual repeating of the request in the face of the child's delay tactics.

Parent: Charlotte, I'd like you to tidy your room today. Grandma is coming to visit this weekend and she's going to share it with you.

Child: I can't today. I'm going out with Brenda.

Parent: I'd like you to tidy your room before you go out.

Child: I don't have time. I promised Brenda I'd be at her house in 20 minutes.

Parent: Call Brenda and tell her you'll meet her after you tidy your room.

Child: (angrily): I can't be late! I promised Brenda I'd be there in 20 minutes.

Parent: (calmly) The sooner you finish cleaning your room, the sooner you'll be able to meet Brenda.

Child: None of my friends have to clean their rooms as often as I do.

Parent: After you finish straightening your room you can go out.

Generally a child will comply with a parent's calm and firm request after three repetitions. The key is not to get pulled off message.

Learning the Hard Way

When my son was in first grade I told him to take his gloves with him when he walked two blocks to the school bus stop. He said he didn't need them. I informed him that it was very cold out but again he refused to take his gloves. I said, "OK, but if your hands get cold it will be very unpleasant." Half-way to the bus stop my son complained, "My hands are freezing." He wanted to go back home to retrieve his gloves and have me drive him to school, since he would miss the bus. I insisted he ride the bus to school as planned, cold hands and all. He would also have to return home on the bus equally uncomfortable.

One of the ways children learn is by living with the consequences or results of their actions or decisions, good or bad. If a favorite toy is left outside too long it will get ruined; when a homework assignment is turned in late, there is a grade penalty; if a teen driver speeds he is likely to get a ticket; if clothes are not placed in the hamper they are not going to be washed. This is called natural consequences because the result is a direct function of a child's behavior and it affects the child only.

Logical consequences result when a child's behavior impacts negatively on others or leads to danger. A teenager borrows the family car and does not come home at the agreed-upon time. As a result he is not permitted to drive the car for a month. These are consequences imposed by parents because the child has abused a privilege. Withholding a privilege such as watching TV or going to the movies with friends on a Saturday night is a discipline practice that works if the privilege is related to a specific misbehavior. "I've repeatedly asked you two to stop fighting over what to watch on TV. I'm getting a headache from all the noise. If you can't resolve your differences in the next five minutes, you'll have to turn the TV off for the rest of the night."

When you impose a consequence for a specific behavior, be sure the outcome relates to your child's action. It does little good to have a teen mow the lawn for a week because he came home after curfew. Keeping a child from going to a party because her room is not clean doesn't make a lot of sense.

Sometimes there are potential consequences you simply want to avoid. If your teenage daughter is having sex with her boyfriend, the natural consequences can be an unwanted pregnancy. You don't want your son to get a DUI (Driving Under the Influence) ever, no matter what lesson this may teach. As a parent you must discuss the legal and personal consequences of harmful behaviors before they occur, making clear what the results will be if the child takes this route. This is not a one-time chat. When it comes to your child's health and safety there must be frequent discussions. This does not mean lecturing or moralizing about inappropriate behavior; rather, what you want to do is help your child make better choices by informing him of the outcome of particular actions.

If you try to spare your child the consequences of his behavior—you do his dirty laundry even if it is not in the hamper, he drives your car even though he didn't live up to the agreement he made with you—you are not allowing him to learn from his decisions, and you keep him from becoming self-disciplined.

Taking a Break

I've never been one to favor time-out as a discipline practice but on occasion, when my son was overly worked up, I'd suggest that he go to his room, get centered, and come out when he was ready to discuss the problem he was having.

Time-out isolates a child for a period of time in response to an unacceptable behavior. The child is sent to her room, or made to sit in a chair in a corner, or is otherwise separated from family members. A timer is sometimes used to mark off the minutes of the separation. Many parents find this technique helpful, although they tend to overuse it. If you choose to use time-out, there are ways to make this technique effective.

• Do not overuse this method by employing it at the slightest provocation. If you do so it loses its effectiveness. Use time-outs for serious misbehavior, such as for hitting a sibling or breaking something in a fit of anger. Time-out also works when a child is agitated or wound up about something and needs to calm down. Sometimes the real problem is that a parent needs a time-out from an energetic youngster. Giving a time-out for behaviors such as refusing to eat or crankiness is not appropriate.

• Talk to your child about time-out when she is not misbehaving. Put the time-out chair where you can see it but away from a view of the television. Show her how the timer works.

• Warn your child before isolating her. "I want you to stop hitting your brother. If you don't you are going to have to sit in the time-out chair."

• Give the child a few seconds to stop what she is doing. If she doesn't, take her to a chair you've designated for time-out. Remind her, "You did not stop hitting your brother. You will have to sit here and think about your behavior." Do not discuss this action with the child; ignore crying, pleading and begging. Do not allow the child to go to the bathroom or the refrigerator.

• Explain the punishment. "You will stand here for _____ minutes." Approximately one minute for each year of your child's age is enough time. Giving a two-year-old a 20 minute time-out will seem like an eternity, and it will often end with the child having a temper tantrum. If the child leaves the timeout chair, return her to it. If need be, stand nearby to make sure the child stays where she is put.

• If you want to give the child an opportunity to be released from time-out, explain what she must do. "When you're willing to watch TV without hitting your brother you may return." If you want the child to stay in time out for the duration of the punishment, when time is up, free the child from isolation with "Now you may go back to playing with your brother."

• When your child returns to her usual activity, praise her for behaving the way you desire. "I'm really happy that you are getting along with your brother."

• If you find you are using time-out excessively, reevaluate what is going on between you and your child. Maybe he doesn't have enough to do and this is why he is getting into mischief. Perhaps he needs more attention from you. It's possible that you need a break from him.

Lighten Up and Tell Tales

Children like to laugh and a parent who uses humor to teach or correct a behavior can defuse a conflict in a way that makes even the most nonreceptive child pay attention. "I think your dirty clothes just got up off the floor and walked away." "If you hand this paper in to Mrs. Wilson you better tell her the dog wrote it." Be sure that your jokes do not ridicule your child or hurt her feelings.

Children also love to hear things about other children. It is a good practice to tell or read stories about youngsters who do positive things.

See No Behavior, Hear No Behavior

Sometimes it is best to do nothing. Train yourself to ignore minor or harmless misbehavior. Your daughters get into an argument over one borrowing the other's hair dryer without asking. Do you really have to interfere in this? Your son comes home from school in a bad mood and slams his book bag on the kitchen table with a loud bang. Let it pass and give him time to be ready to talk to you about his troublesome day. If you focus on the book bag you may miss out on what's important. Like adults, children get agitated for any number of reasons and the annoyance passes quickly. The less attention you give to minor behavior breaches, the more energy you'll have for important problems.

Knowing When To Fold

I have a friend whose parents insisted that he and his twin sister attend church services with them every Sunday. My friend and his sister refused to go to church once they reached adolescence. They said they didn't believe in organized religion and weren't going be a part of one, not an unusual adolescent stance. The twins argued with their parents every Saturday and Sunday and were often punished for their refusal to go along with their parents' beliefs. Both children left home as soon as they were financially able.

Sometimes there is a values or belief clash so strong between a parent and a child that no amount of discussion is enough to change a child's mind. If the action doesn't involve illegal activity or danger, as in drug use, it makes no sense to argue, fight, punish or otherwise force a child to see things your way when he or she is adamant about something. Your daughter is going to keep the green streak in her hair (for a while anyway), your son is going to quit college to work at a ski resort for a year because his girlfriend is there, your toddler fastens her mouth closed to avoid eating vegetables. As difficult as it may be, you sometimes have to back off and let things be if you want to preserve your good relationship with your child.

Ultimately, It's Do As I Do

When he was 17, my son discovered a large, black-and-white photo of his late father, taken when his father he was in his 20s. I made the mistake of having the photo framed and giving it to my son as a gift. My son hung it in his bedroom. The problem was, the young man in the photo had struck a movie star pose, a cigarette in his hand, a stream of smoke rising from it. Within a few weeks of getting the photo, my son took up smoking. While there may have been other reasons for my son's behavior—many teens think smoking is "cool"—I have always felt that this new habit had a lot to do with my son imitating his father.

Children learn by observing the behavior of others. They expand their knowledge and develop skills by seeing and listening to the people around them, in effect, learning vicariously how to act in the world. While considerable learning takes place from direct experience, an exceedingly important phenomenon (known as modeling or observational learning) enables children to learn without having to do things directly. The most influential models for children are parents. If you want your child to internalize your values, you must first examine your own behavior.

It is by watching and listening to their parents that children learn how to display anger, express love, treat other people, and problem-solve. They pick up on parental values by seeing what is important to their parents. If you want a kind and considerate youngster, treat your child and others with respect. If you want a responsible child, be dependable and trustworthy yourself.

One of the most important things you can teach your child in life is to put himself in another person's place and understand how that person is feeling. This is called empathy. Parents who discipline their children by pointing out the effect of their misbehavior on others are more likely to get empathetic children than parents who focus on the behavior alone. "Samantha is sad because you took her toy," has a different effect than, "You were bad for taking that toy." Empathy in children is particularly shaped by modeling and imitation, in seeing how the adults around them act in response to the distress of others.

Compassion, thoughtfulness and helpfulness are the by-products of empathy. Kind children come out of thoughtful homes. They see their parents do good deeds—collect food for the homeless at Thanksgiving, take an elderly neighbor to a medical appointment, participate in a marathon race for a charity; the opportunities to help others are endless. Letting children help cook, take care of animals, water the plants, assist a sibling with homework and do other considerate things in daily life give them a sense of self-worth, particularly when such positive behavior is rewarded with praise. In the long run, the way you teach your child to treat others is the way he or she will treat you.

Chapter Thirteen
RESTLESS GHOSTS REVISITED

*The adult in our time is asked to reach his or her hand
across the line and pull the youth into adulthood. If the
adults do not turn and walk up to this line and help
pull adolescents over, the adolescents will stay exactly
where they are for another twenty or thirty years...*

Robert Bly
The Sibling Society

One of English literature's most famous love affairs occurred
between the poets Robert Browning and Elizabeth Barrett.
What makes the relationship so extraordinary was that the
lovers, well into their thirties, had to meet in secrecy for a
year before fleeing to Italy in 1846, where they married and
had a son, Pen. The reason for the deception was Elizabeth's
father, Edward, who forbid his children to ever leave him
and who disowned and disinherited any of his sons and
daughters who married. Although she did manage to leave
her father's home, Elizabeth was unable to emotionally
distance herself from him enough to live a happy, productive
adult life. After her marriage she kept her father's picture by
her bedside and sent him pleading letters, which he never
opened. Overtaken by a mysterious illness, probably psychological in origin, Elizabeth retreated into invalidism and an
addiction to morphine. She died at the age of 54, leaving her
beloved Robert to raise their 12-year-old son alone.

On some level all parents feel like Edward Barrett,
reluctant to let their children go when the time comes.
But the impulse to be a restless ghost in your children's lives
must be resisted. Your kids reach adulthood: They go to

202

college, get a job, join the military, move in with friends, marry, travel across the country, or take any one of endless opportunities available to them. This can be a difficult time, especially if an adult child continues to rely on you for financial support or if, as is occurring more frequently because of the economic realities of modern life, he or she continues to live at home. Your role as a parent must change if you want your child to emerge from the transitional years of adolescence as a happy, competent and caring adult. You must form a new relationship with him or her, one based on equality and the mutual respect any two adults are expected to show each other.

> *The shift toward adult-to-adult status requires a mutually respectful and personal form of relating, in which young adults can appreciate parents as they are, needing neither to make them into what they are not nor to blame them for what they could not be. Neither do young adults need to comply with parental expectation and wishes at their own expense.*
>
> Betty Carter and Monica McGoldrick
> *The Changing Family Life Cycle*

Letting Go In Stages

Family life is built upon entrances and exits, departures and returns, losses and gains, all changes that must be negotiated in a way that moves children forward. How you respond to the separation that comes with a child reaching adulthood depends upon the success of earlier stages. If you do not let go gradually, and in appropriate ways, you may find yourself in a relationship with an overly dependent adult or a grownup rebel angrily breaking away from parental control in a strike for independence.

In reality, good parents begin letting go of their children in early childhood as youngsters strive for a level of autonomy that begins with things like choosing their own clothing, deciding what they want to eat, and developing friendships outside the family.

Parents who view their years with their children as successful continue to be supportive and interested in their children as the children move on to their adult lives. They also anticipate new opportunities in their own lives.

In a world where an increase in life expectancy makes it likely you will need assistance from your children at some point, it seems especially important that the relationship between you and your children be harmonious and satisfying. The reward for the hard work you have done as a parent is the joy of looking back on the wonderful experiences that are a part of raising sons and daughters, and looking ahead to the love and friendship that comes when a close and caring relationship exists between you and your grown children.

INDEX

A

Adolescence
  brain changes 132–133
  dating 143
  growth spurt 127
  homicide rate 18
  hormonal changes 125
  daily rhythms 130
  early development 128
  identity formation 134-137
  late development 129
  parents' influence 145–146
  peer group 118
  physical ills 127
  problems 149–150
  stages of development 125
  sexuality 131
  suicide rate 18
  teens and depression 18
  teens and pregnancy 18
Adolescent thinking 133
  imaginary audience 133
  personal fable 134
  pseudostupidity 134
Adolescents and work 139
Adult alcoholics 20
Afterbirth expectations 60—61
Age-appropriateness 97
American culture 79

B

Baby's first year 63-64
Bedwetting 69
Brazelton, T. Berry 39

C

Child abuse and neglect 19
Children and friendship 118–123
  popular children 118
  neglected children 118
  rejected children 118
Children's emotional expression 160, 162
Children's manners 104
Children's mistakes 67
Clinton, Bill
  childhood 67–68, 90
  Clinton, Virginia 67
  Clinton, Roger 67
Communication in families 159–160
  communication techniques 162–165
  techniques that encourage talking 103
Competence in children 106
  the importance of school
  learning skills 107
Connectedness and separateness 79

D

Decoding social cues 114

Definition of caring children 20
Definition of competent children 20
Definition of happy children 20
Definition of parent 22
Definition of parenting 22
Determinants of good parenting 22–23
Discipline vs. punishment 171
  effects of hitting and spanking 176
  link between violence and child maltreatment 19
  techniques to avoid 188
  name-calling 66
  negative labels 66
Discipline as problem solving 180–186
  discipline without conflict 186–200
  logical consequences 195
  "I" messages 192
  plain speaking 193
  the problem with punishment 172–176
  time-out technique 197
  using humor 198
  modeling behavior 200
Divorce in the family 87–91
  children's reaction to divorce 88
  factors determining the outcome of divorce for children 88
  good divorce 89—90
  separation 88
  second marriages 91

E

Early childhood changes 63, 97–98
  temper tantrums 69
  safety issues 104
  routines 104
Edelman, Marian Wright
  childhood 20
Elimination problems 46
Elkind, David 133–134
Emotional response to children 61
  parent's anger 61—63
Empathy 201

F

Factors that influence parenting 46
Family bed 100
  family bed alternatives 102
  family bed dangers 101
Family harmony 69—70
Family of origin 85—86
Family meetings 165–166
Family systems 70
  enmeshed families 82-83
  infantilized child 75—76
  roles and rules 76–77
  disengagement in families 83
  parentified child 73–74, 75—76
  triangulation 83-84

Financial costs of having a child 28–32
  US News and World Report 29
Friendly home 121

G

Ginott, Hiam 162

I

Importance of school 138
Infant development 97–99
  brain development 97
  crying 116
  cues 114
  dependence 80
  reading to babies 99
Innate differences in children 36-37
  genes and the environment 43
  genes and their effect on behavior 36–37,
  40–41, 43, 114
  personality differences in children 37–38

K

Kerry, John
  childhood 33-34

L

Language development 102
  techniques that encourage talking 103
Letting go in stages 201
Life changes for parents 25–26

M

MacArthur, Douglas
  childhood 20
  MacArthur, Pinky 20
Mazlish, Elaine and Faber, Adele 163
Middle childhood changes 64
  self-care 105
  making comparisons 107
My Big Fat Greek Wedding 81

P

Parent's beliefs 59-61
  distorted thinking 61–62
  "right" and "wrong" issues 65
  parent's anger 61–63
  parents as mind-readers 65
  magnifying and miminizing 65
Parent's self-awareness 46
  life changes 25
  the person of the parent 45
Parent-adolescent conflict 140–141, 143
Parenting as a science and art 62
Parenting as a bidirectional process 33, 42
  fun of parenting 60-61
  niche-picking 40
  narcissism in parents 46
  negative emotions 66
  responsiveness and demandedness 45

stress and parenting 46
Parenting myths 60—62
Parenting styles 51–57
  authoritarian parenting 51–52
  authoritative parenting 53–54
  permissive indulgent parenting 52–53
  permissive neglectful parenting 53
Parents and school 138–139
  school success 106–107, 109
Peer groups 118
Play 117, 121
  interpersonal play 117
  symbolic play 118
  playing with infants 99
Prebirth expectations 59

R

Resilient children 110
  promoting resiliency 110
Rivera, Geraldo
  childhood 124–125
Roosevelt, Eleanor
  childhood 152–153

S

Seligman, Martin 112
Self-esteem in children 107
Self-image in children 106
Simon, Carly
  childhood 113–114
Social skills 120
Stages of development 64–65
Steinberg,Lawrence 145
Spielberg, Steven
  childhood 44–45, 49
  Spielberg, Leah 44–45, 49
Steinem, Gloria
  childhood 21
  Steinem, Ruth 21
Stepparenting 91–93
  stepparenting role 92–95
  stepparents' relationship 95
  stepparent and stepchildren's relation-
  ship 95–96
  successful stepparenting 92–93
Stress and parenting 46

T

Tasks of parents 23–24, 61
Temper tantrums 69
The Measure of Our Success 21
"Terrible twos" 63

W

Wright, Orville and Wilber
  childhood 77–78